Food Haikus

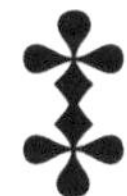

by

Koh An Ting

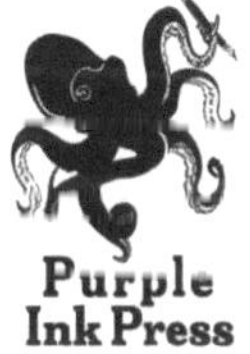

**Purple
Ink Press**

San Diego,
California

Purple Ink Press
6977 Navajo Road, Unit 414
San Diego, California, 92119
www.purpleinkpress.com

Food Haikus / Koh An Ting. -- 1st ed.
ISBN 979-8-9892793-6-4

Cover image by Koh An Ting
Cover design and interior design by Koh An Ting and Yael Aldana

Dedicated to Kozue

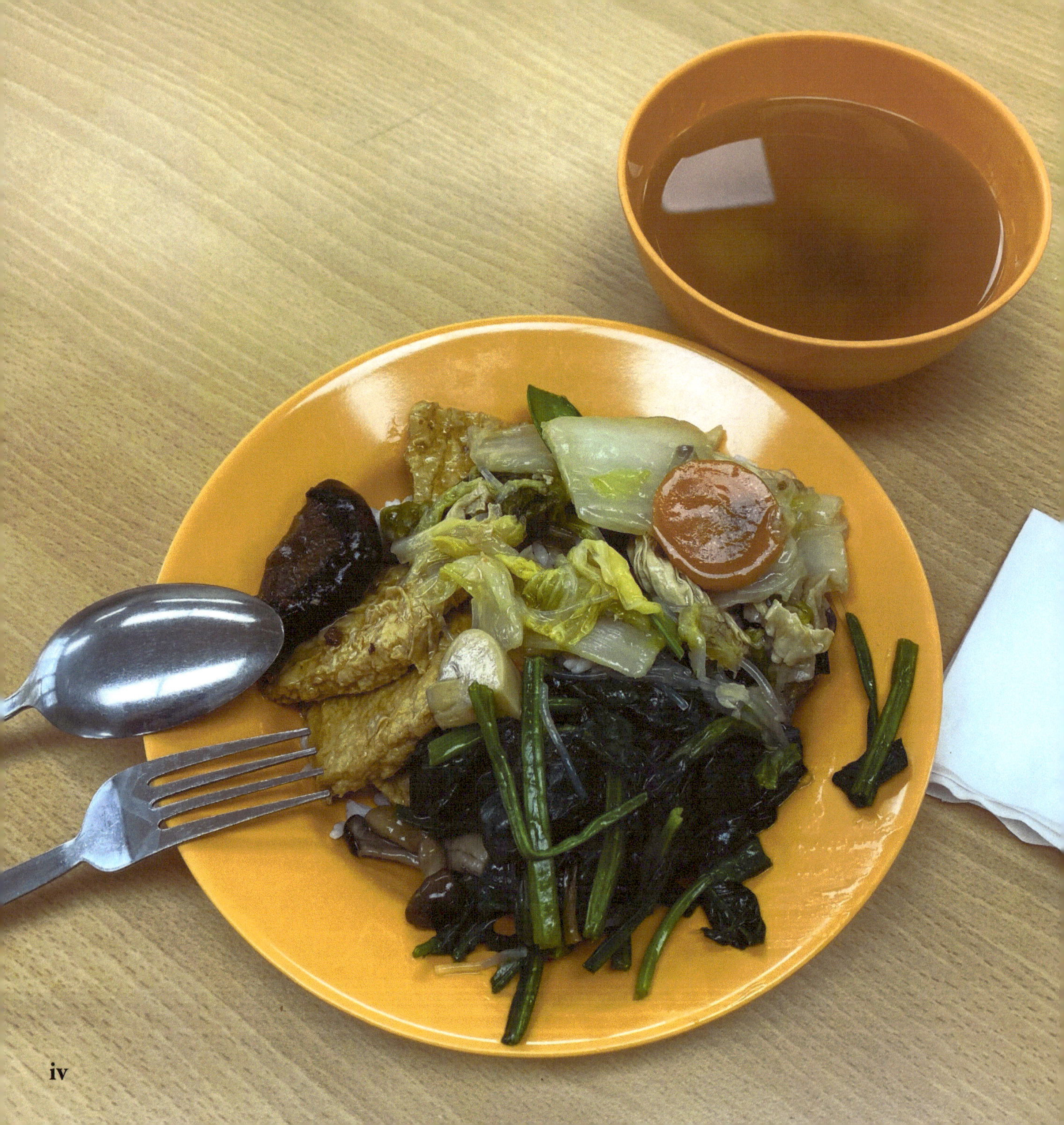

Table of Contents

An Ting's Introduction to The Collection

I was thrilled when Purple Ink Press announced their chapbook contest in 2024, declaring that "We are doing things a bit differently: We hate binaries." As a non-binary girl (or demi-girl) living in a conservative country, it's been difficult growing into myself. When I saw that they were looking for "weird", and by weird, they meant "idiosyncratic language and attention", that became the impetus for me to compose my first collection for their contest.

The inspiration for this collection is two-fold: my love for Singaporean food, and my love for my girlfriend. As someone growing up in the digital age, I am interested in the merging of visuals and text, both crucial elements, each supporting the other. It also seems apt that, as my girlfriend is Japanese, the haikus are almost an ode to her homeland, a homage to her culture.

Zen masters have traditionally used haikus to convey a lot in very little, with every haiku possessing multiple layers of meaning, awaiting the keen reader to peel them off, layer by layer, like a multilayered kueh lapis, a traditional dessert found in Southeast Asia. As a poet, I am interested in conveying both my love for local cuisine and also adding a layer of subtext—the love for my partner, within the constraints of 17 syllables.

My country, Singapore is an interesting country, a blend of both the old and the new. In this little chapbook, there are haikus featuring hawker food and Western cuisine such as crepes, fish and chips, and oat lattes. Hawker food is on the verge of extinction; it is commonly known that elderly hawkers encourage their children to work as lawyers or doctors, with their recipes dying with them. Both types of food are integral to the modern Singaporean diet and are consumed daily without much thought.

To write these poems, I carefully selected some of my favourite foods from iconic locations across the country.

My creative process was as follows: I travelled there, ordered the dish, then snapped a quick photo before putting aside my mobile phone, then mindfully partaking in each morsel of food. After savouring every bite, I then composed the poem in front of my empty plate, choosing every word as carefully as the chef chose his ingredients for my meal.

In addition, food also ties us to family. Apart from those poems inspired by my partner, others speak to my family connections. In Asia, food and family are inextricable. Instead of saying "I love you", which is almost never heard of, our parents ask us, "Shall I cook for you?" or "Come eat at home, don't eat out" as a sign of their affection toward us.

I hope this collection provides you as much pleasure as it has provided me.

~ Koh An Ting

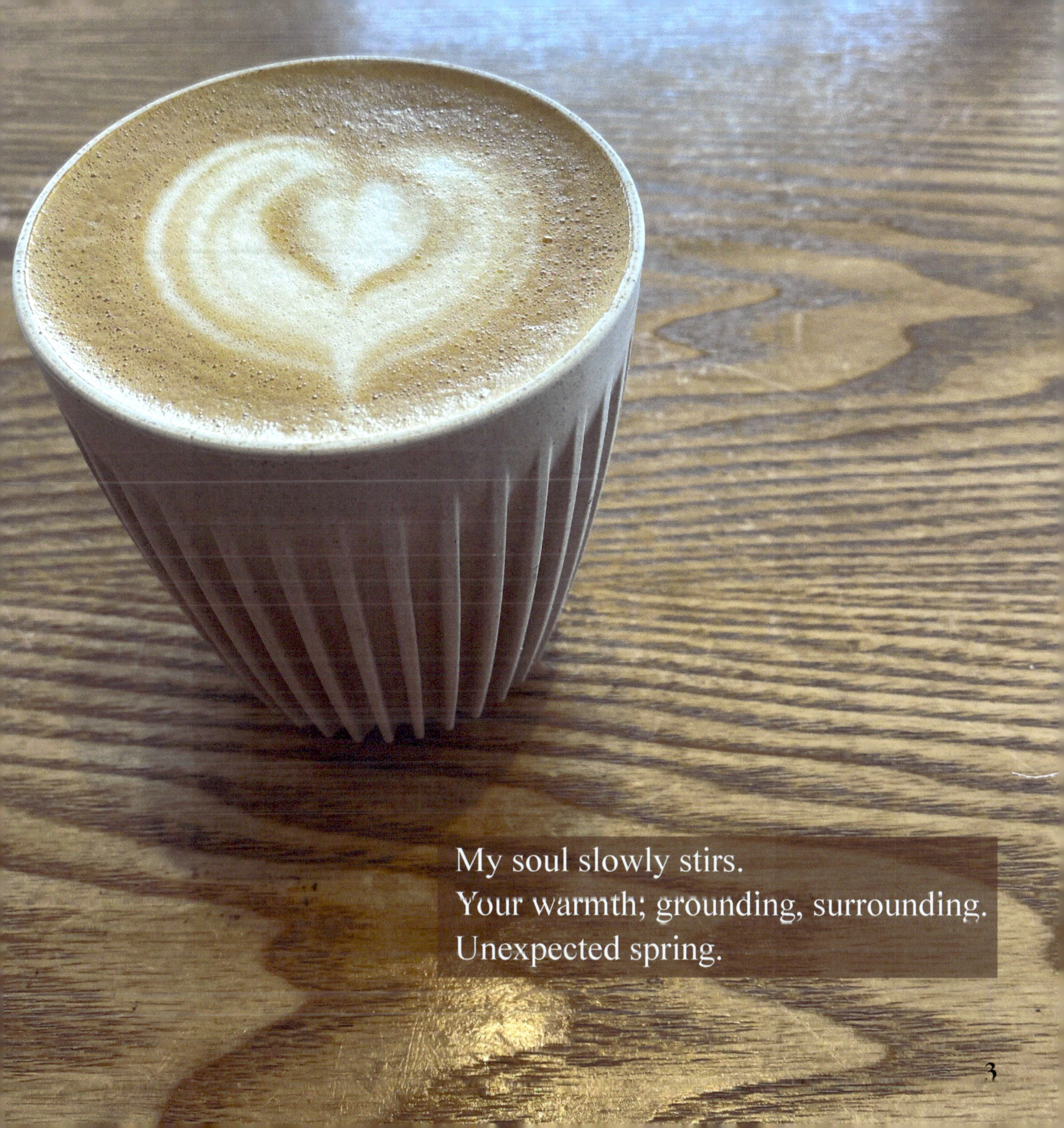
My soul slowly stirs.
Your warmth; grounding, surrounding.
Unexpected spring.

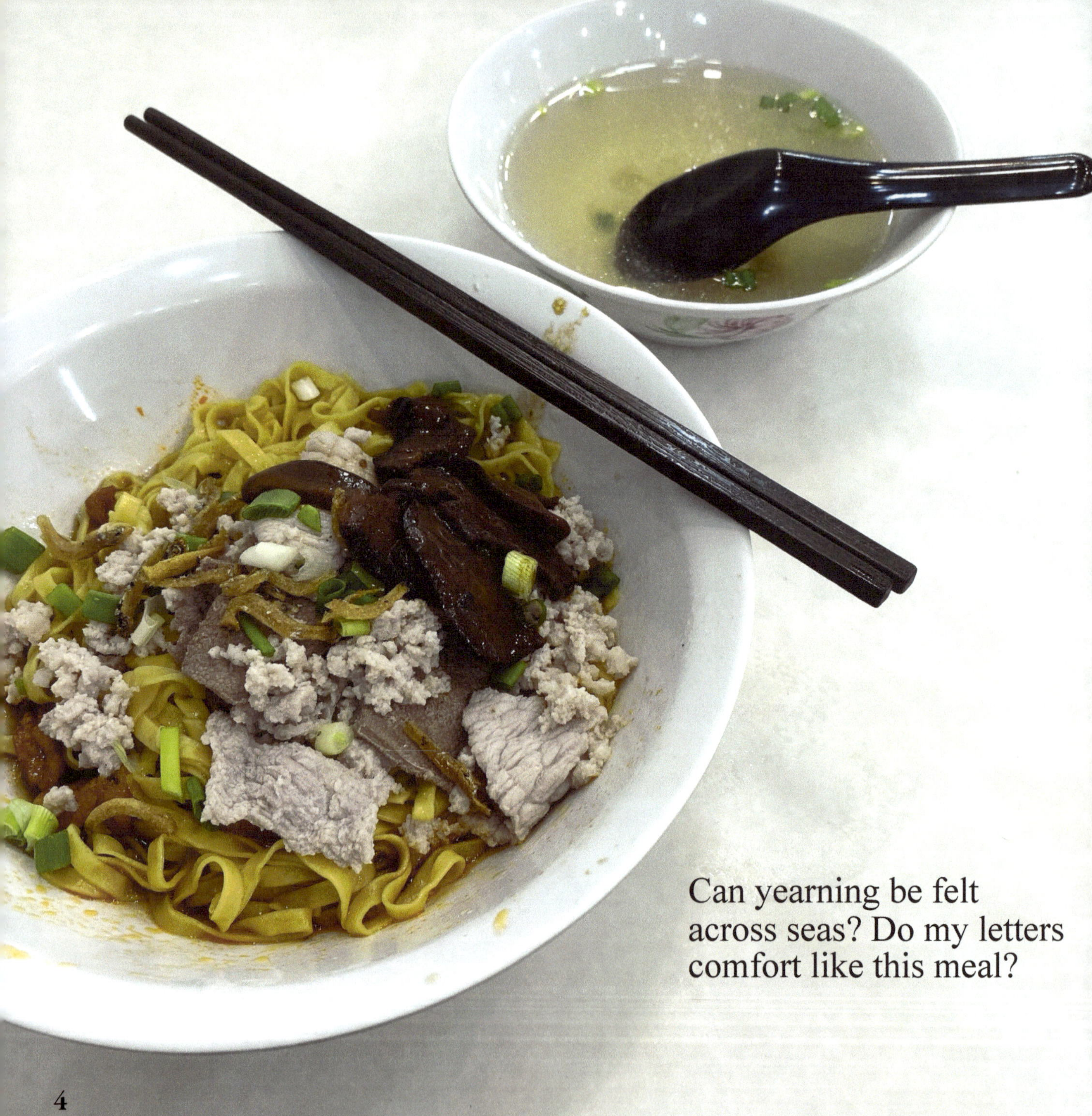

Can yearning be felt
across seas? Do my letters
comfort like this meal?

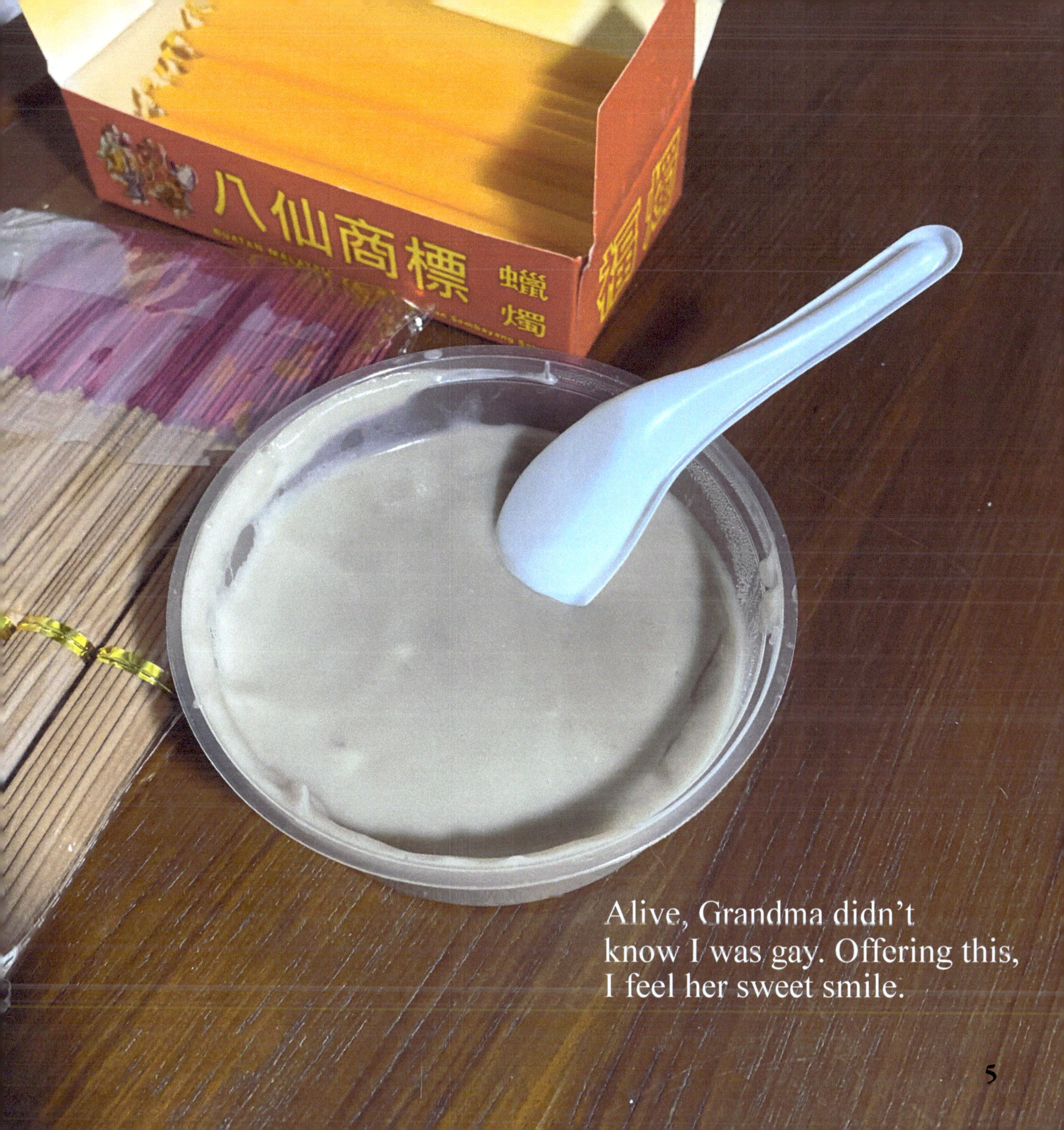
Alive, Grandma didn't
know I was gay. Offering this,
I feel her sweet smile.

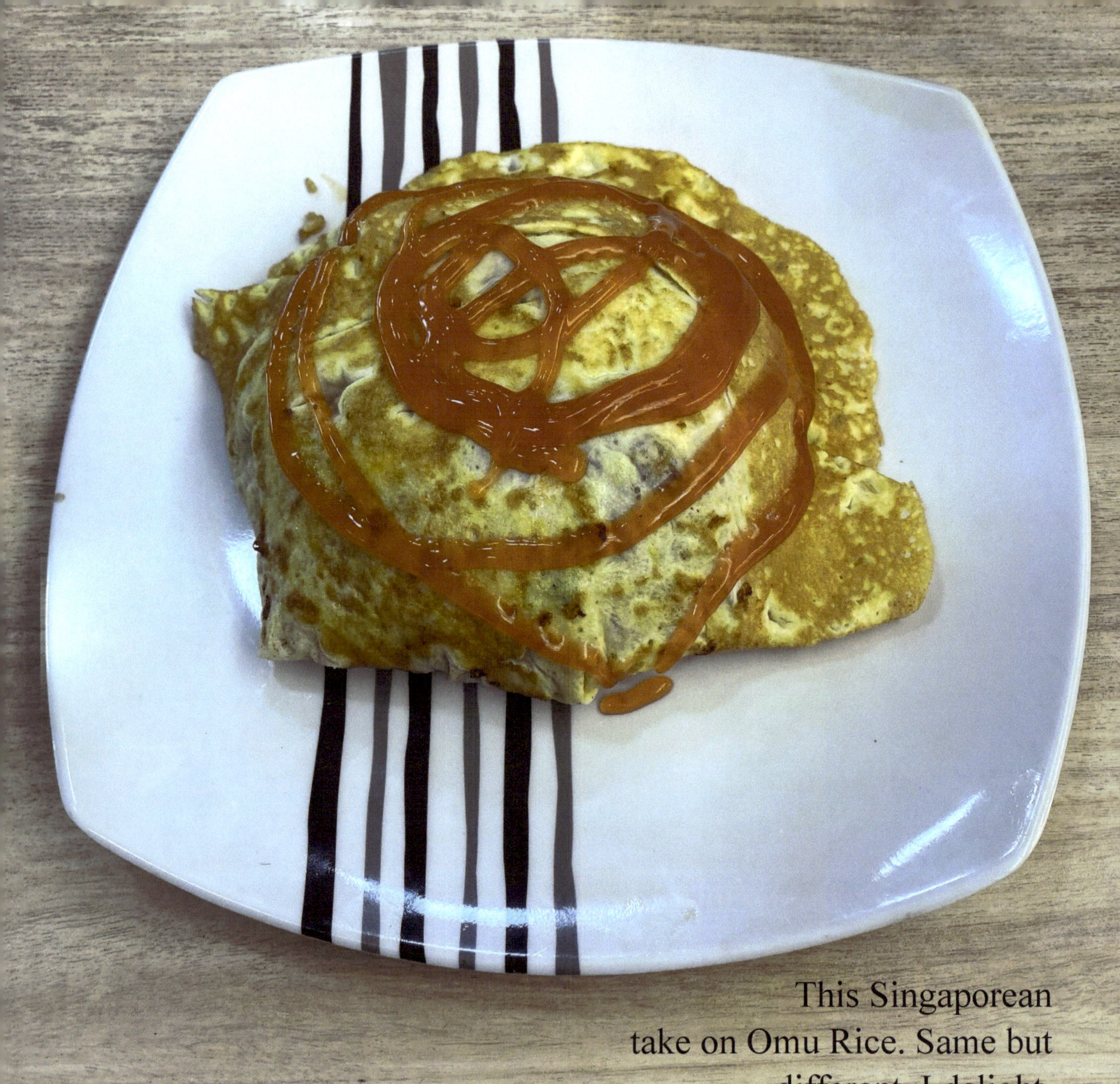

This Singaporean take on Omu Rice. Same but different. I delight.

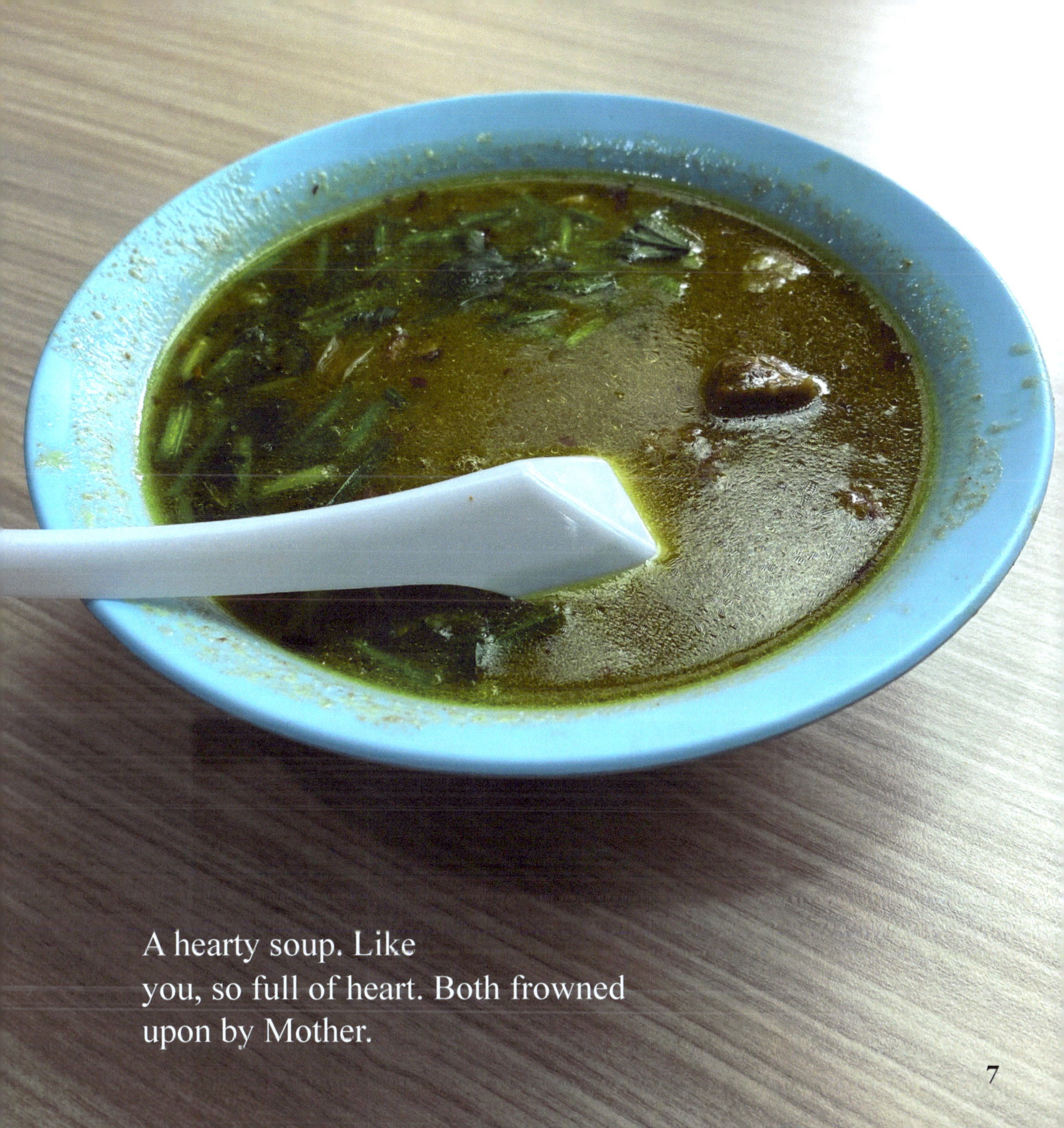

A hearty soup. Like
you, so full of heart. Both frowned
upon by Mother.

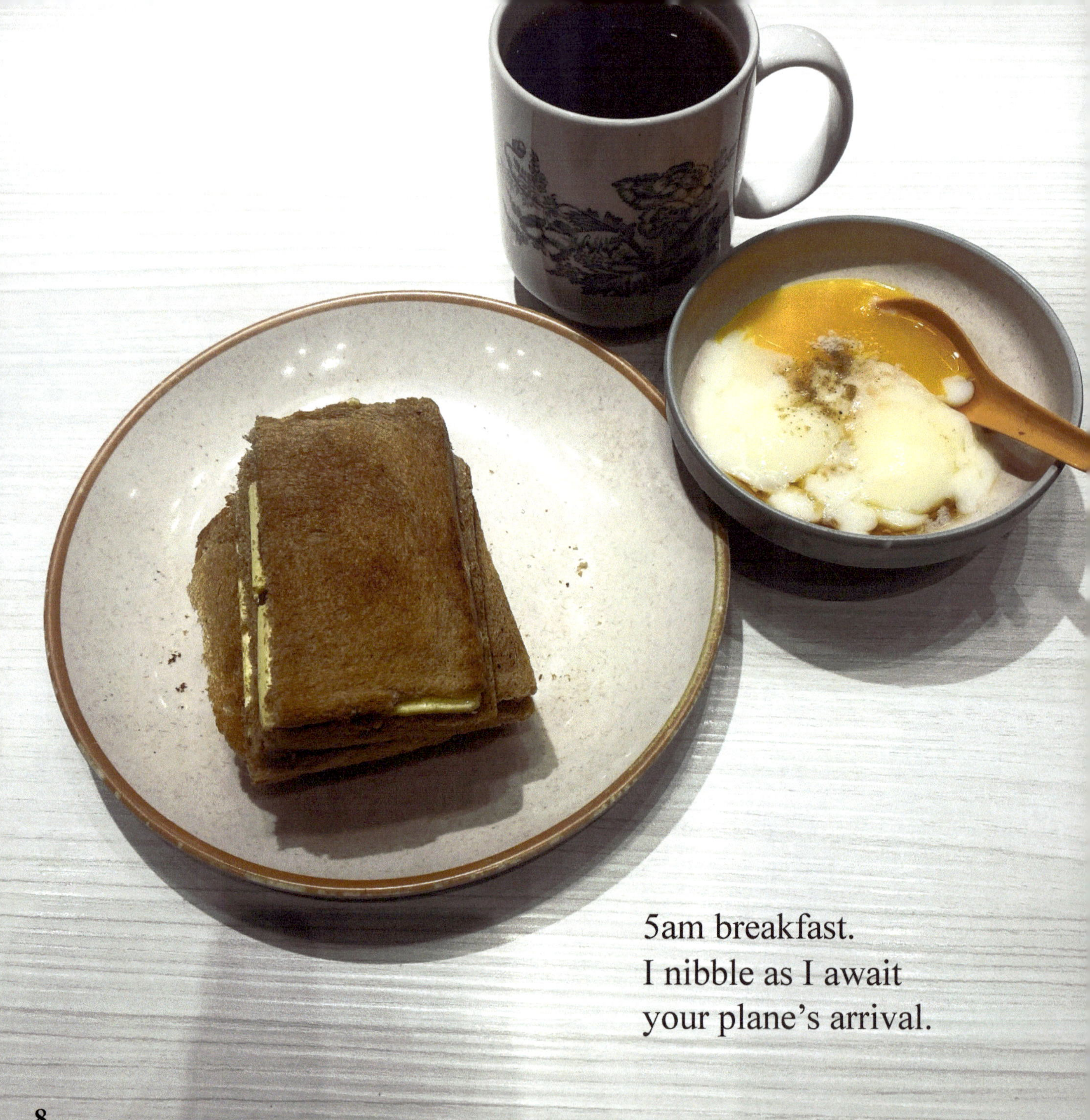

5am breakfast.
I nibble as I await
your plane's arrival.

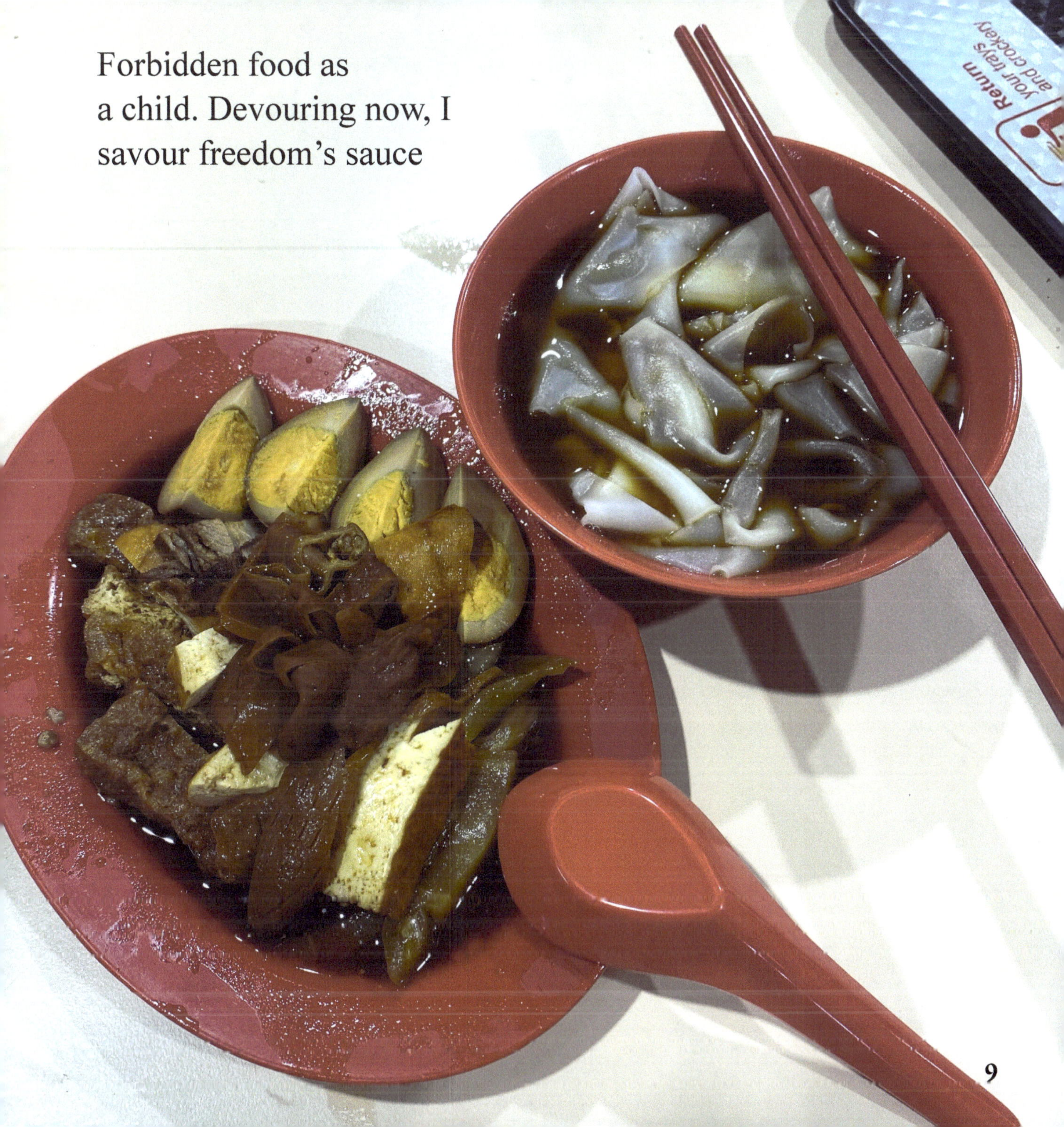
Forbidden food as
a child. Devouring now, I
savour freedom's sauce

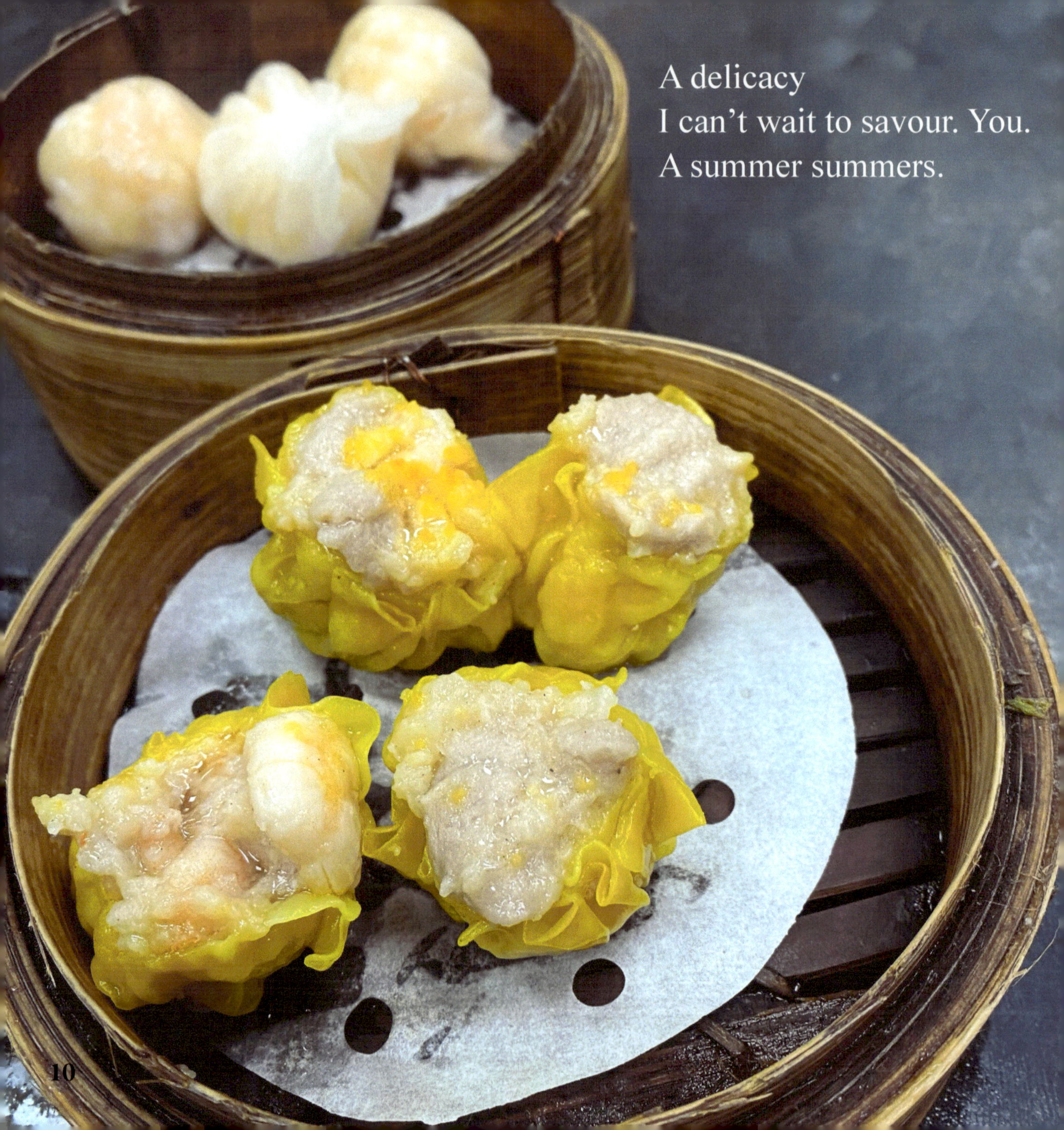

10

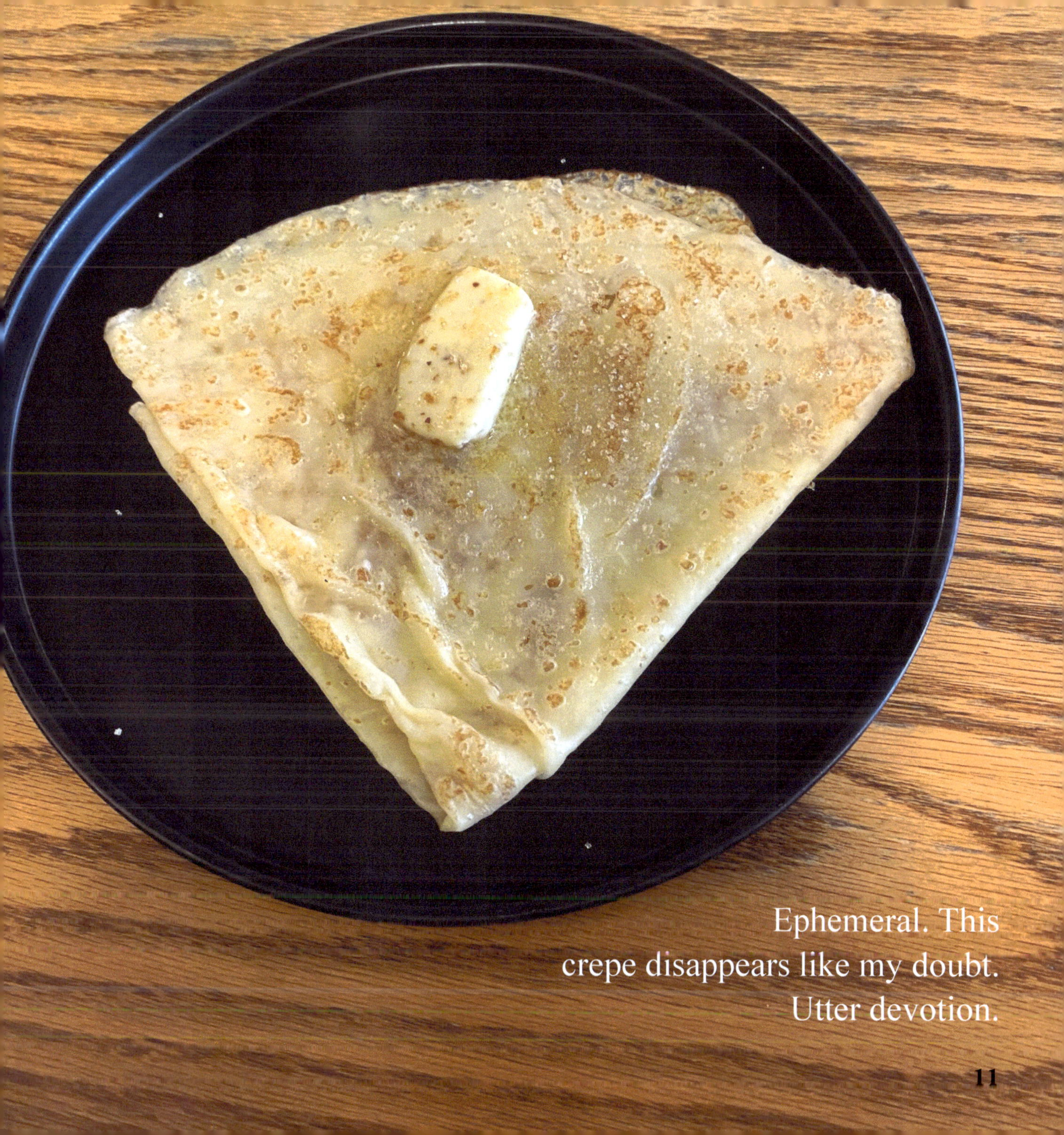
Ephemeral. This
crepe disappears like my doubt.
Utter devotion.

11

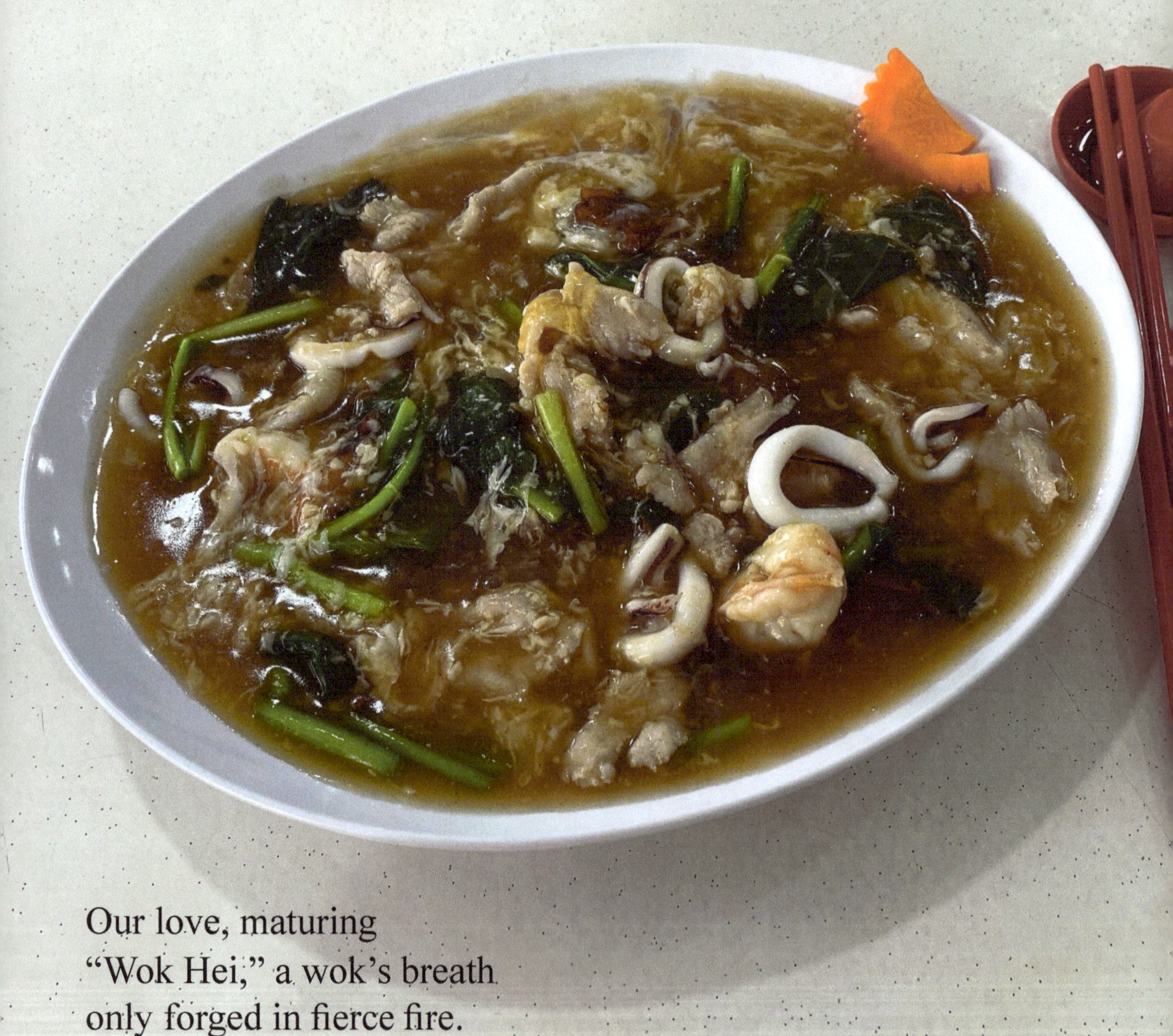

Our love, maturing
"Wok Hei," a wok's breath
only forged in fierce fire.

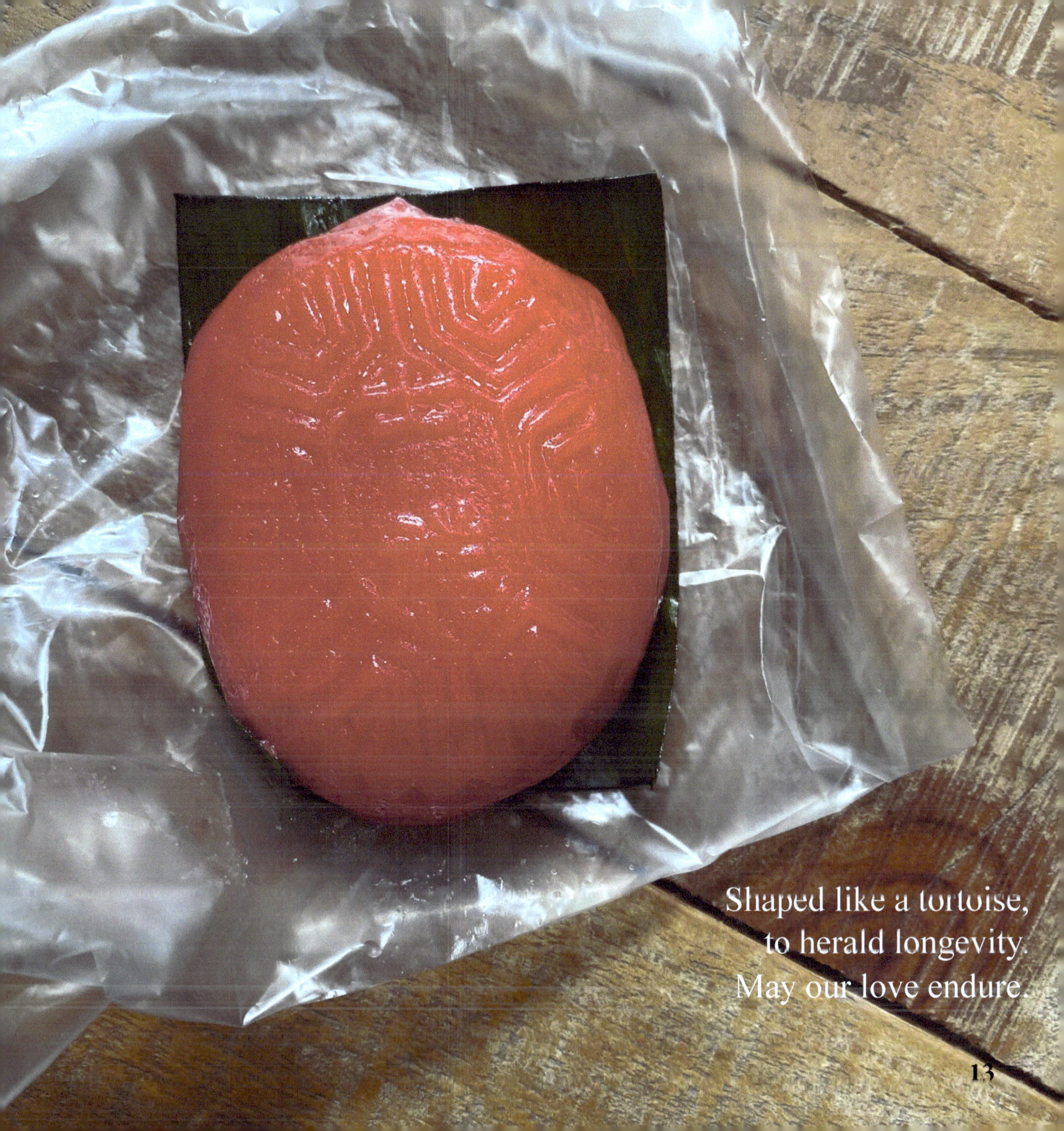

Shaped like a tortoise,
to herald longevity.
May our love endure.

13

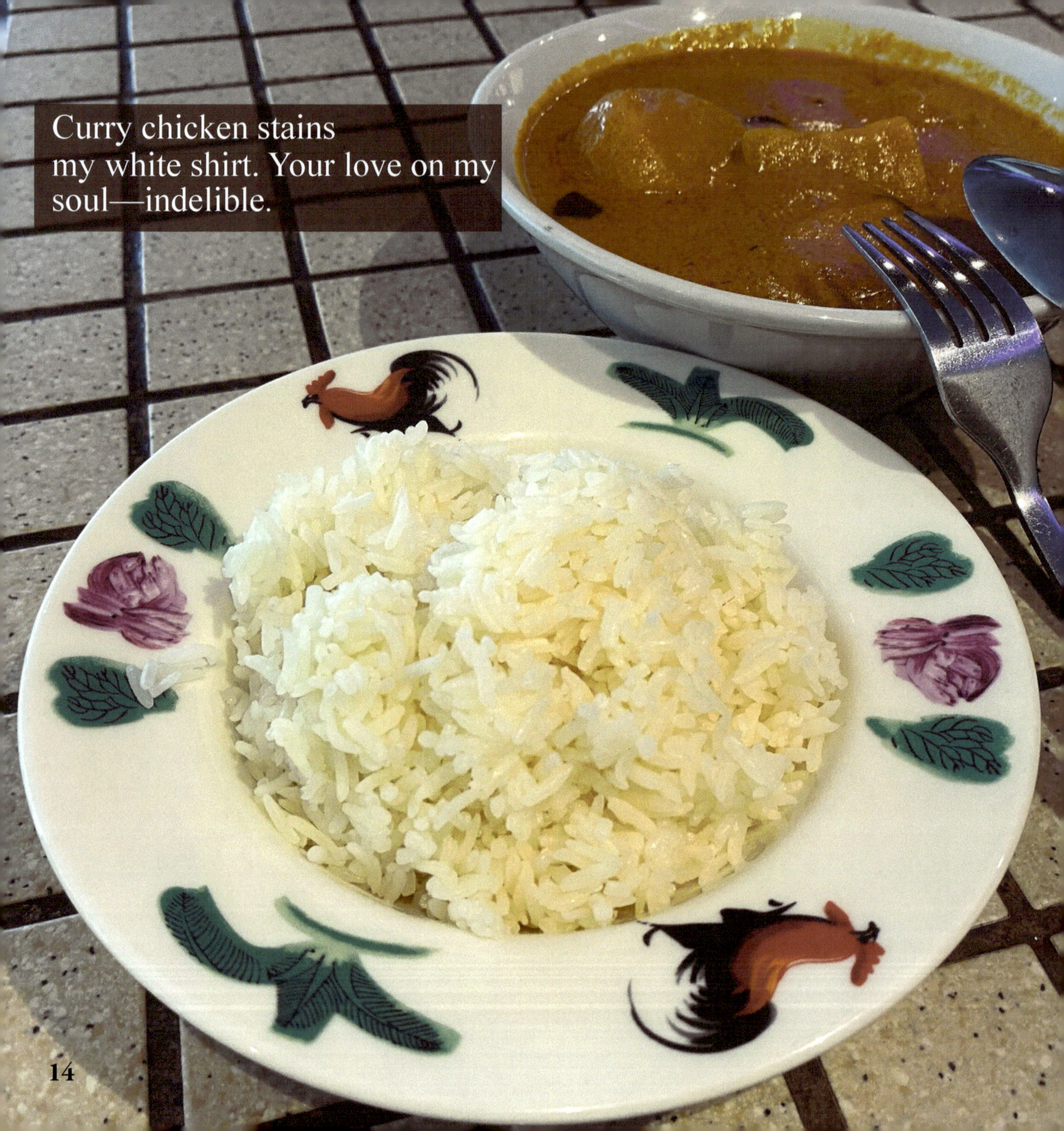
Curry chicken stains
my white shirt. Your love on my
soul—indelible.

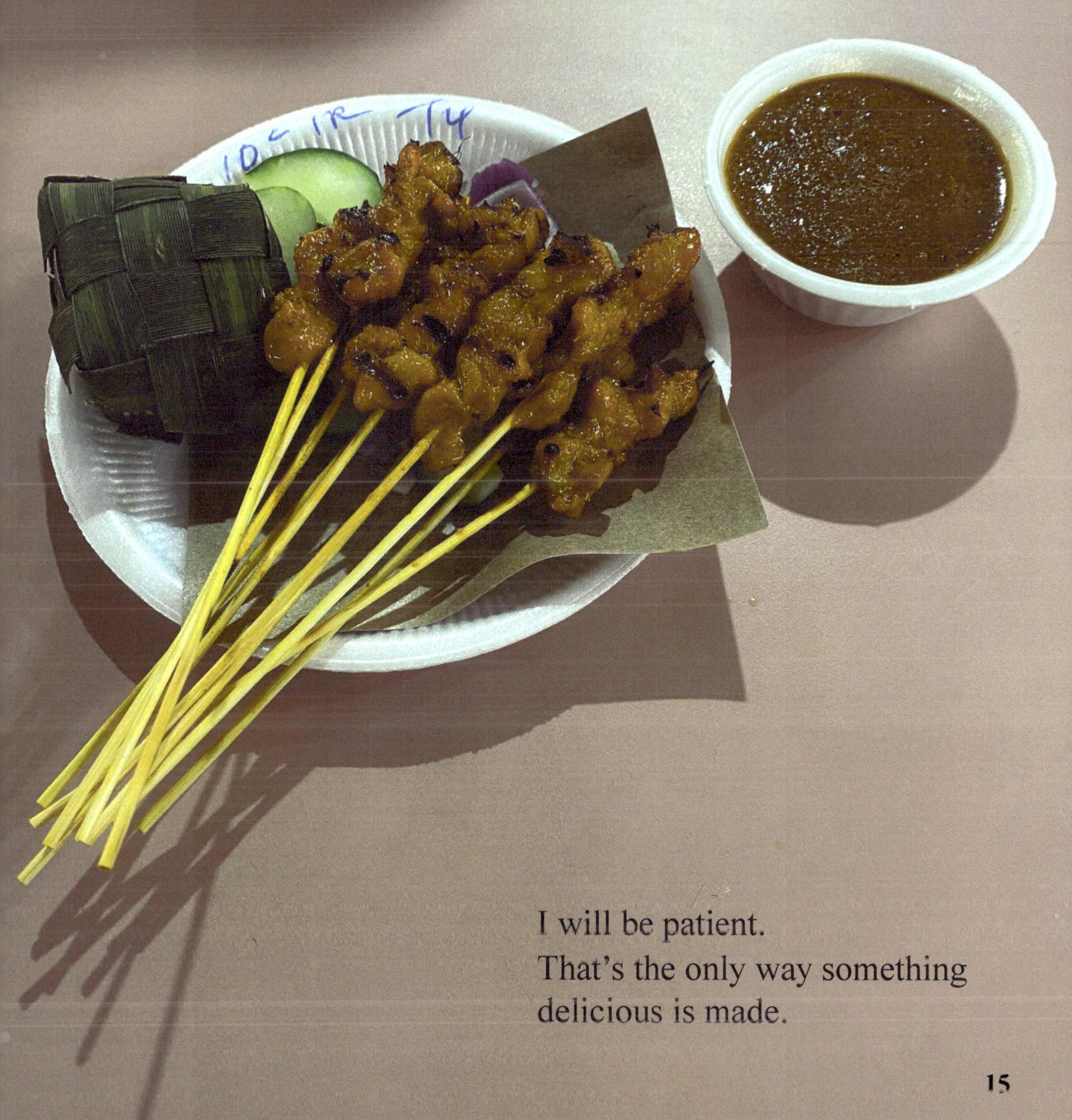

I will be patient.
That's the only way something
delicious is made.

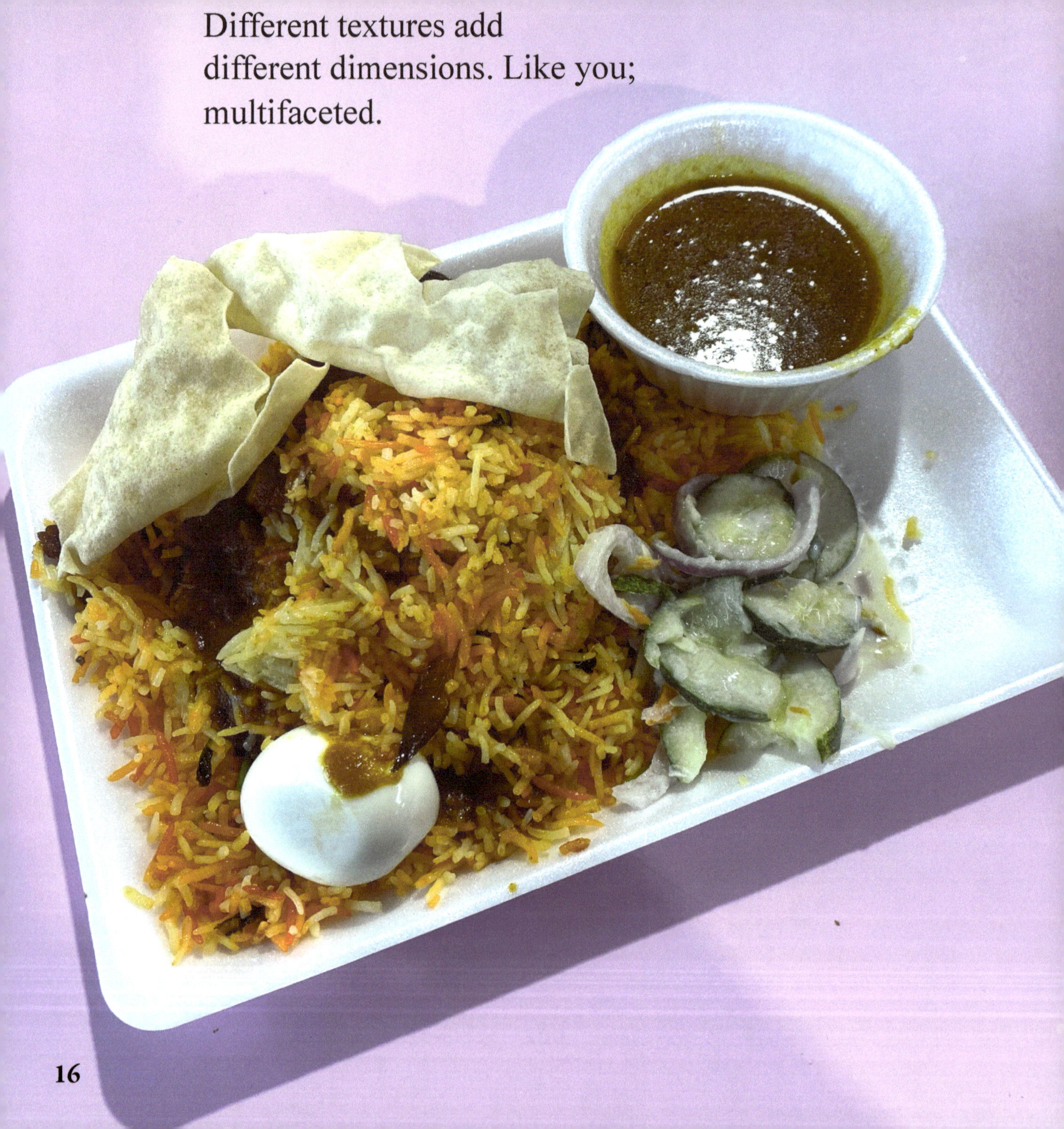

Different textures add
different dimensions. Like you;
multifaceted.

16

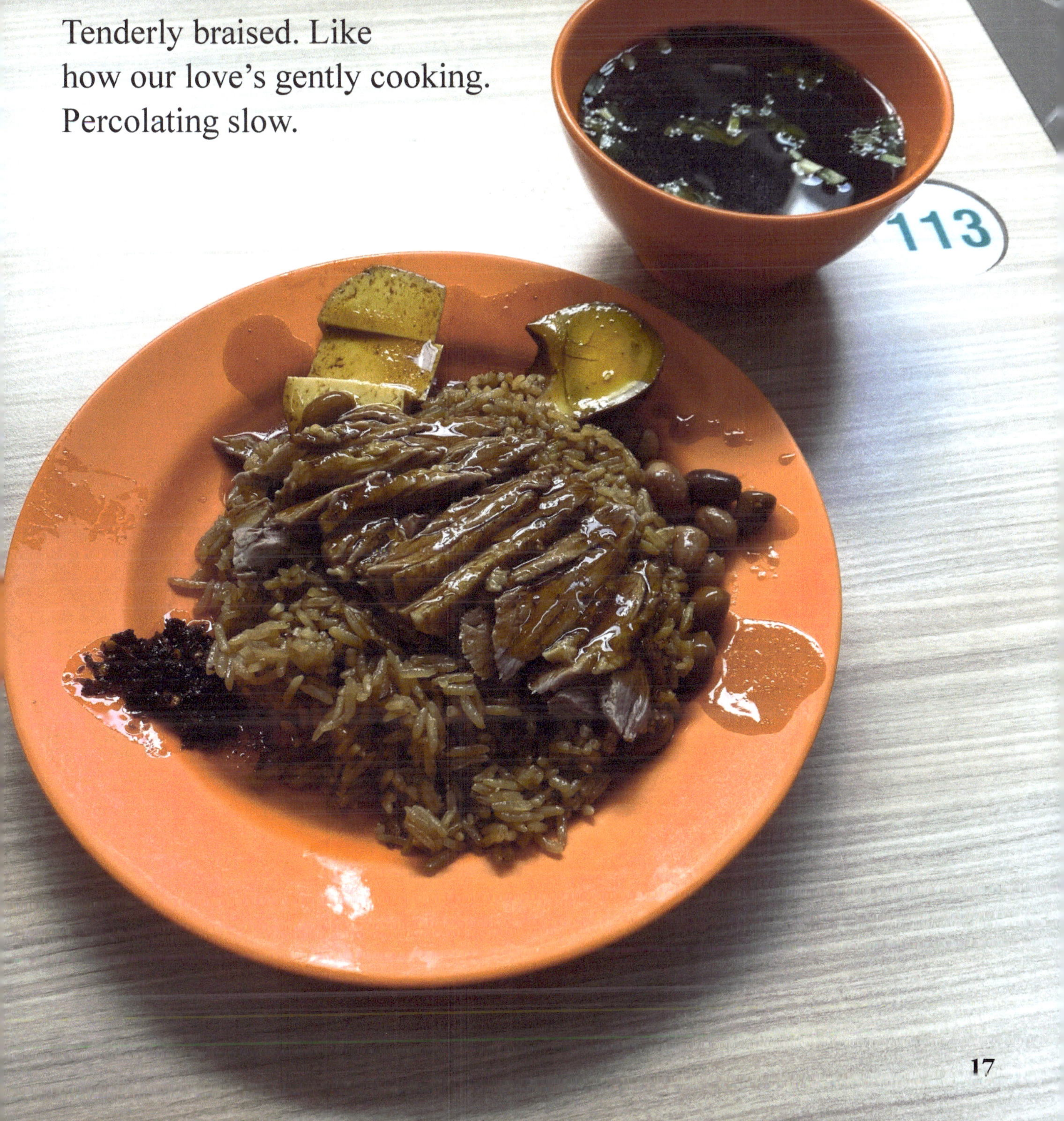

Tenderly braised. Like
how our love's gently cooking.
Percolating slow.

113

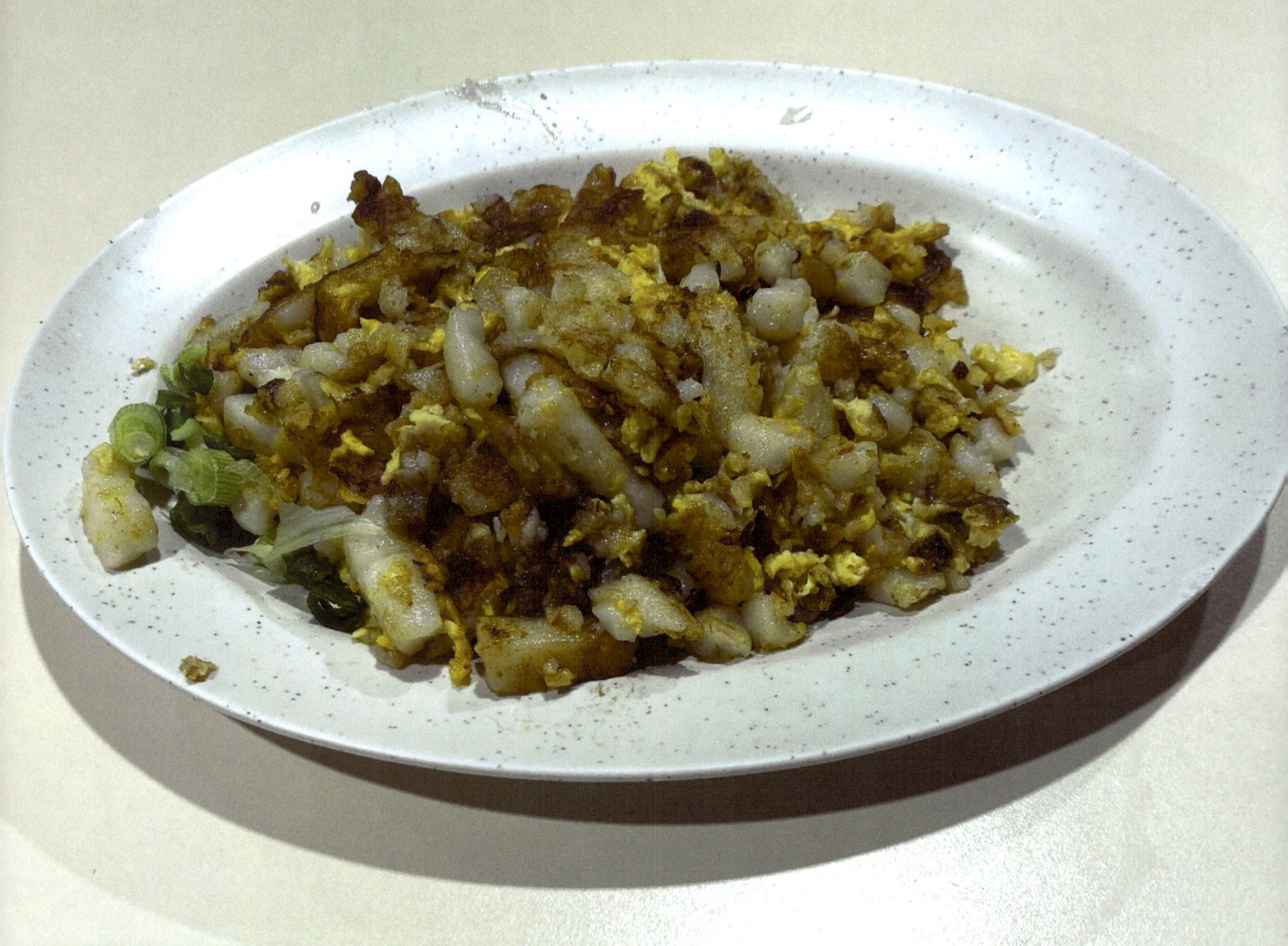

The complexity
of you. The layered flavours.
I'll never tire of.

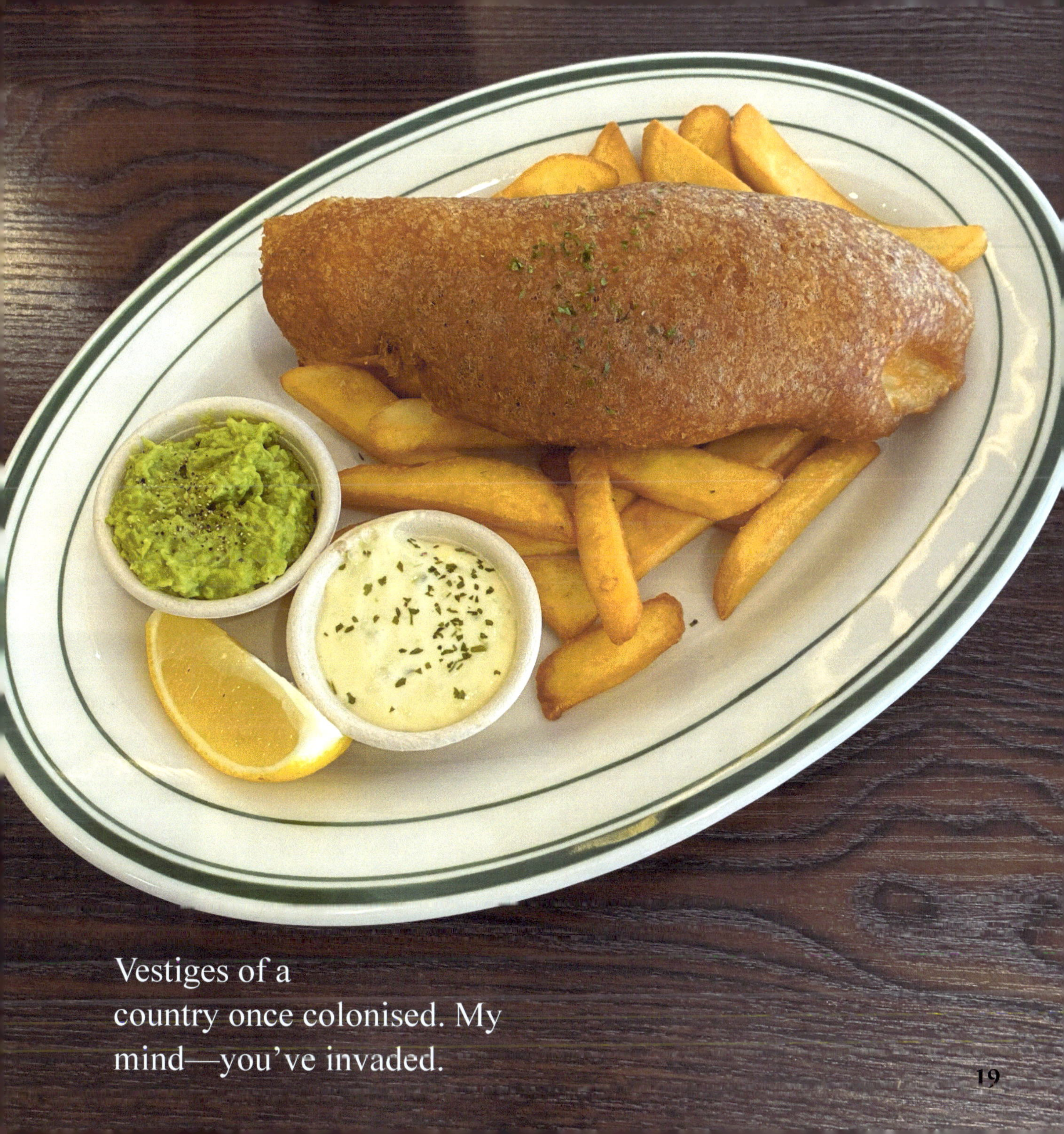

Vestiges of a
country once colonised. My
mind—you've invaded.

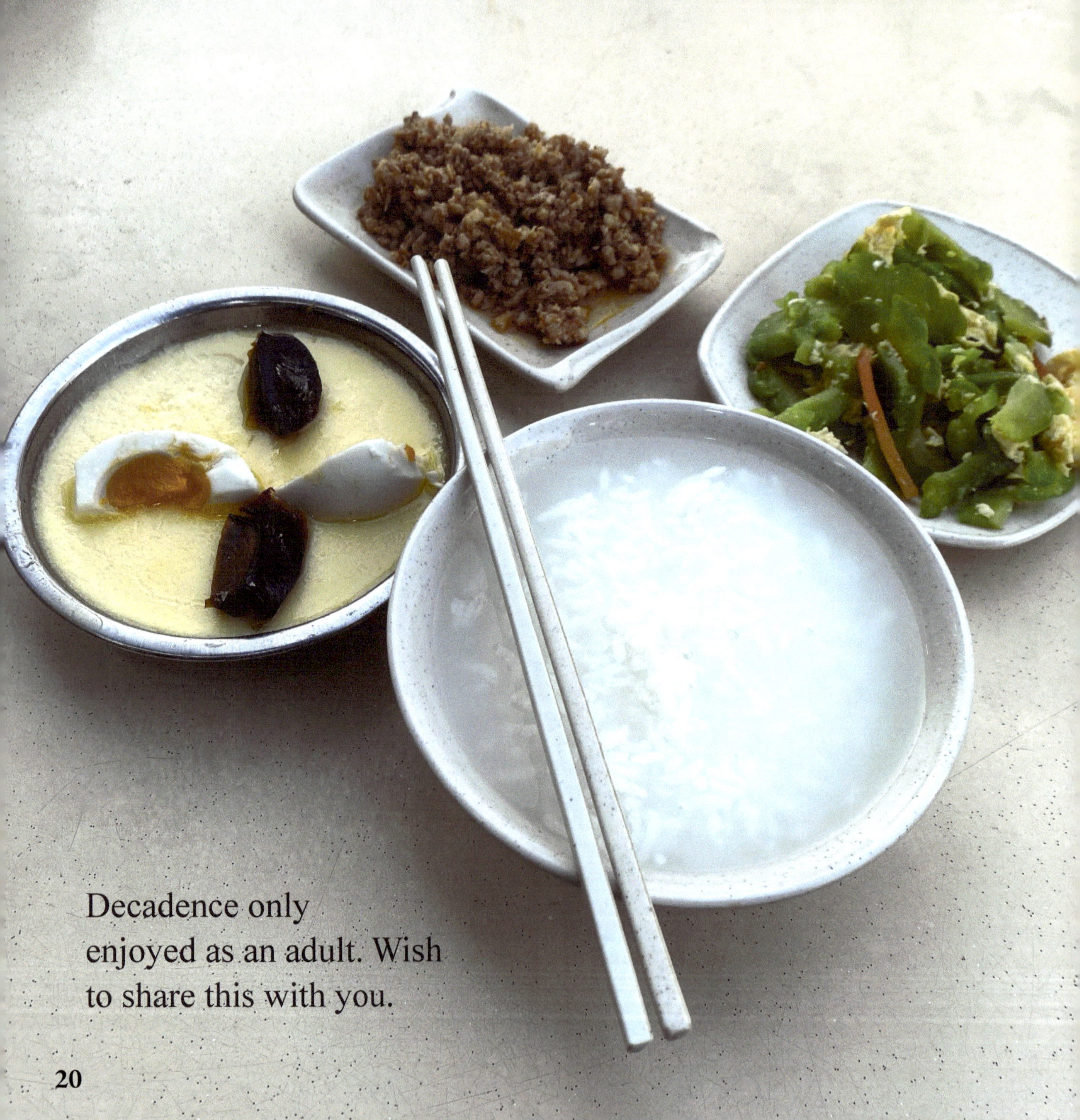

Decadence only
enjoyed as an adult. Wish
to share this with you.

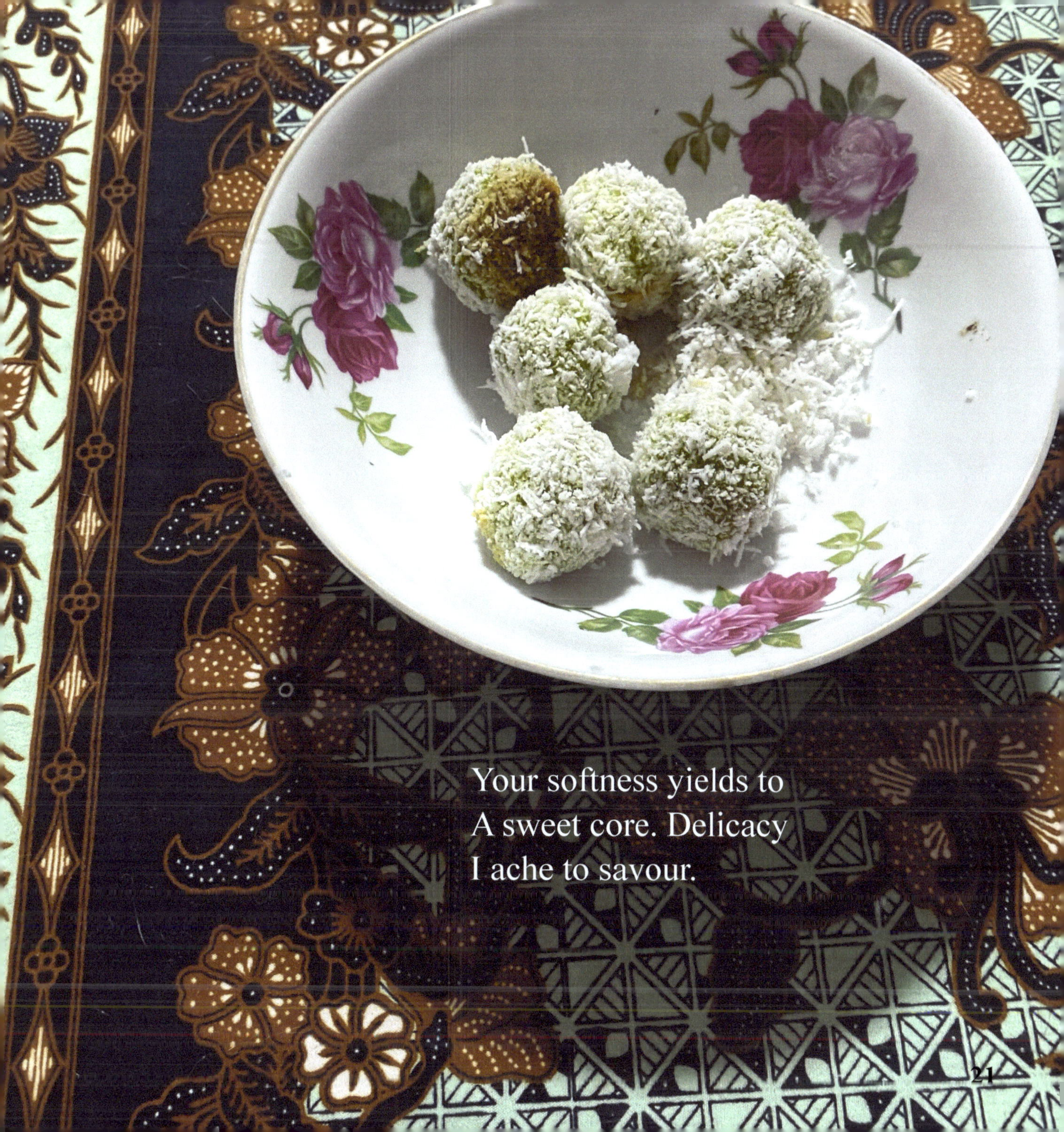

Your softness yields to
A sweet core. Delicacy
I ache to savour.

Second Servings—
A Glossary of Food
found in
Singapore

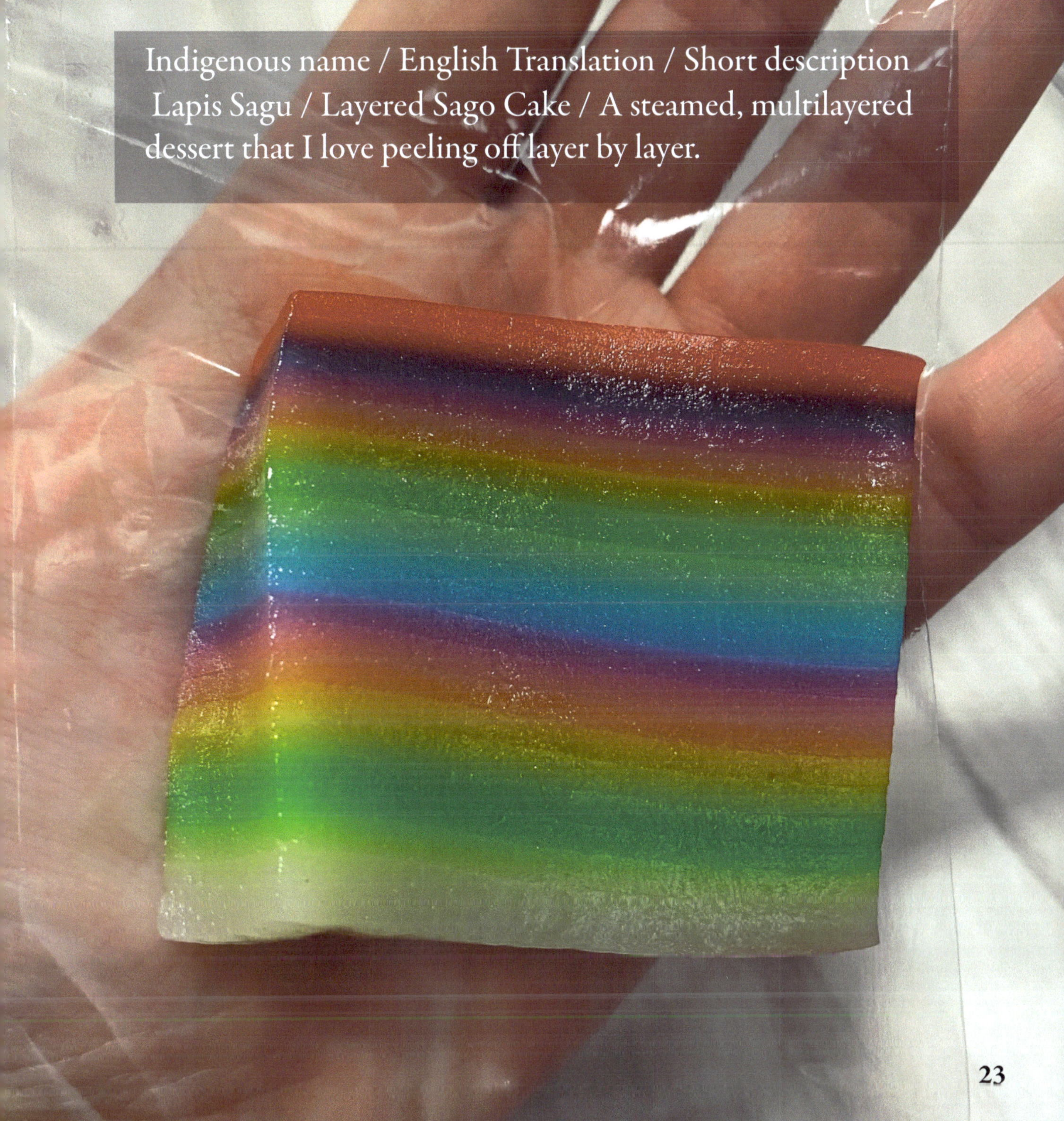

Indigenous name / English Translation / Short description
Lapis Sagu / Layered Sago Cake / A steamed, multilayered
dessert that I love peeling off layer by layer.

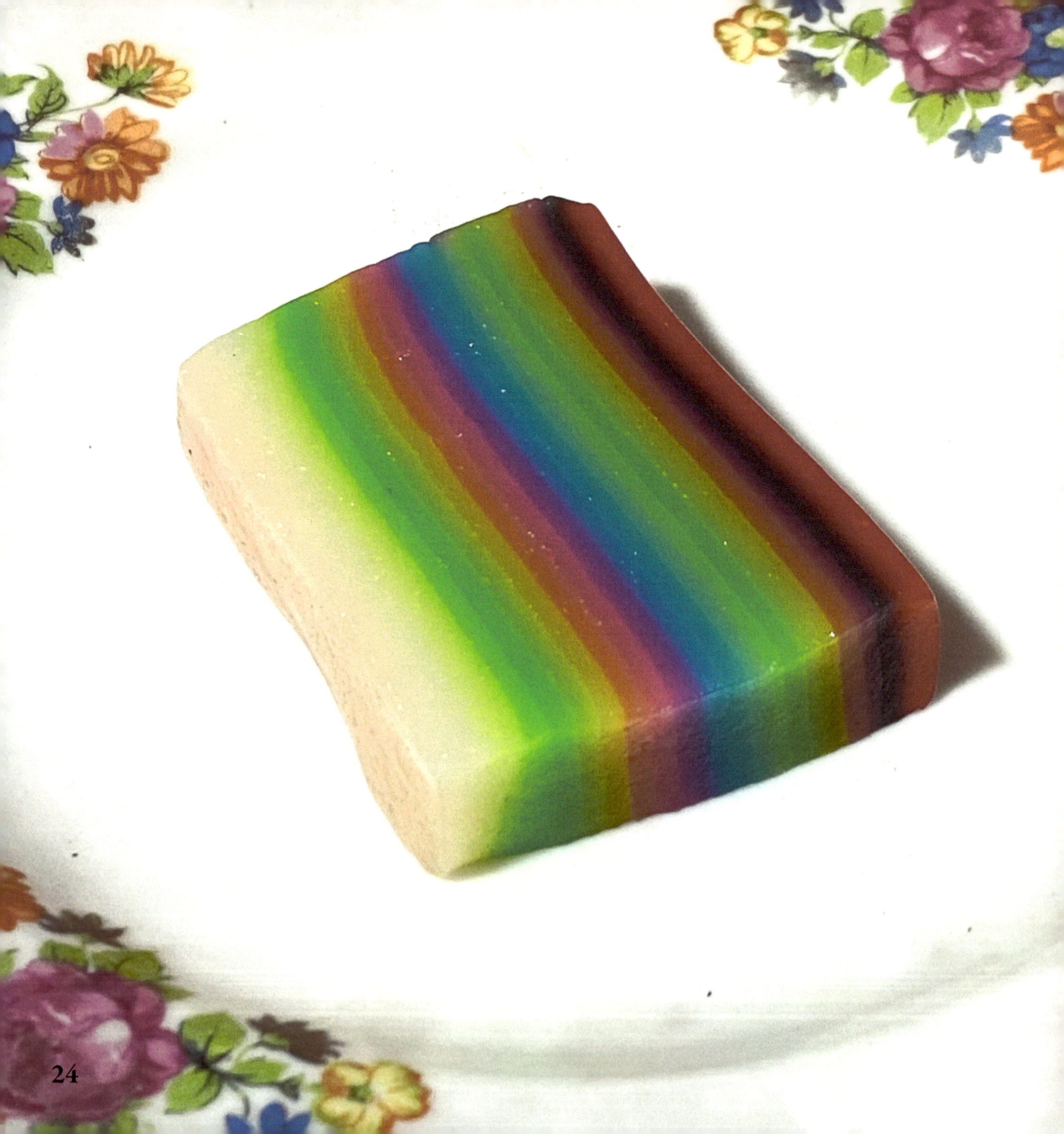

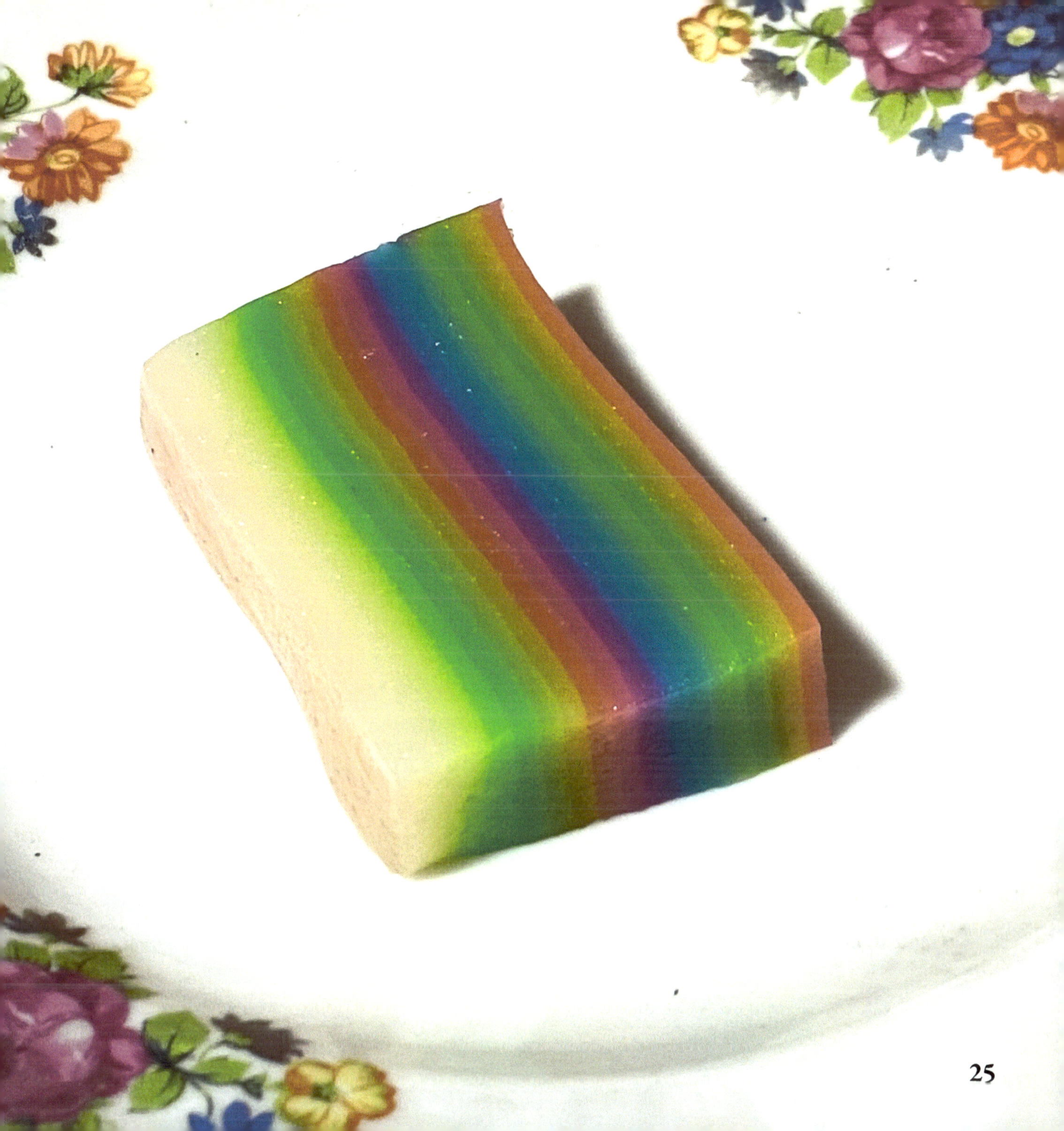

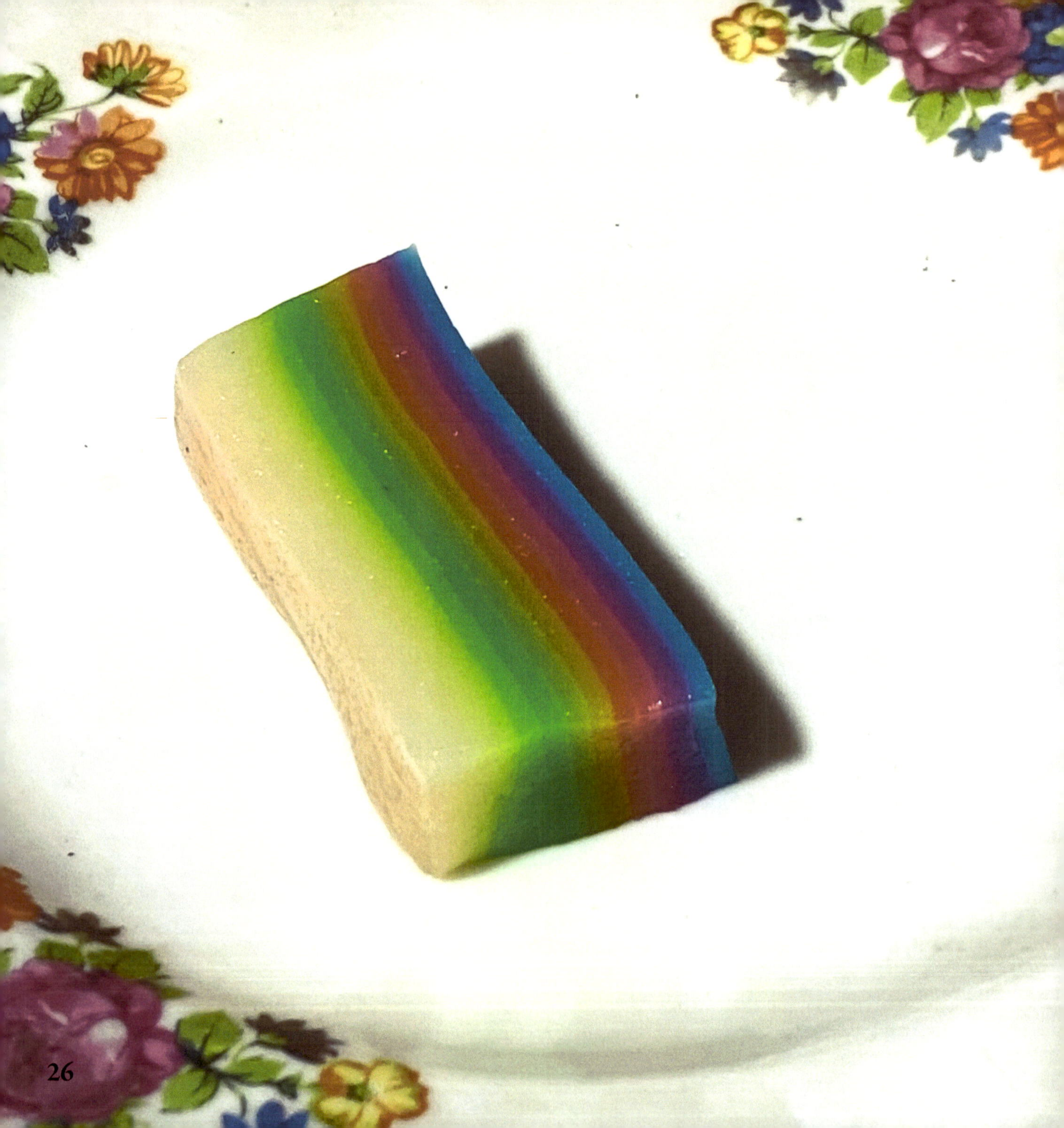

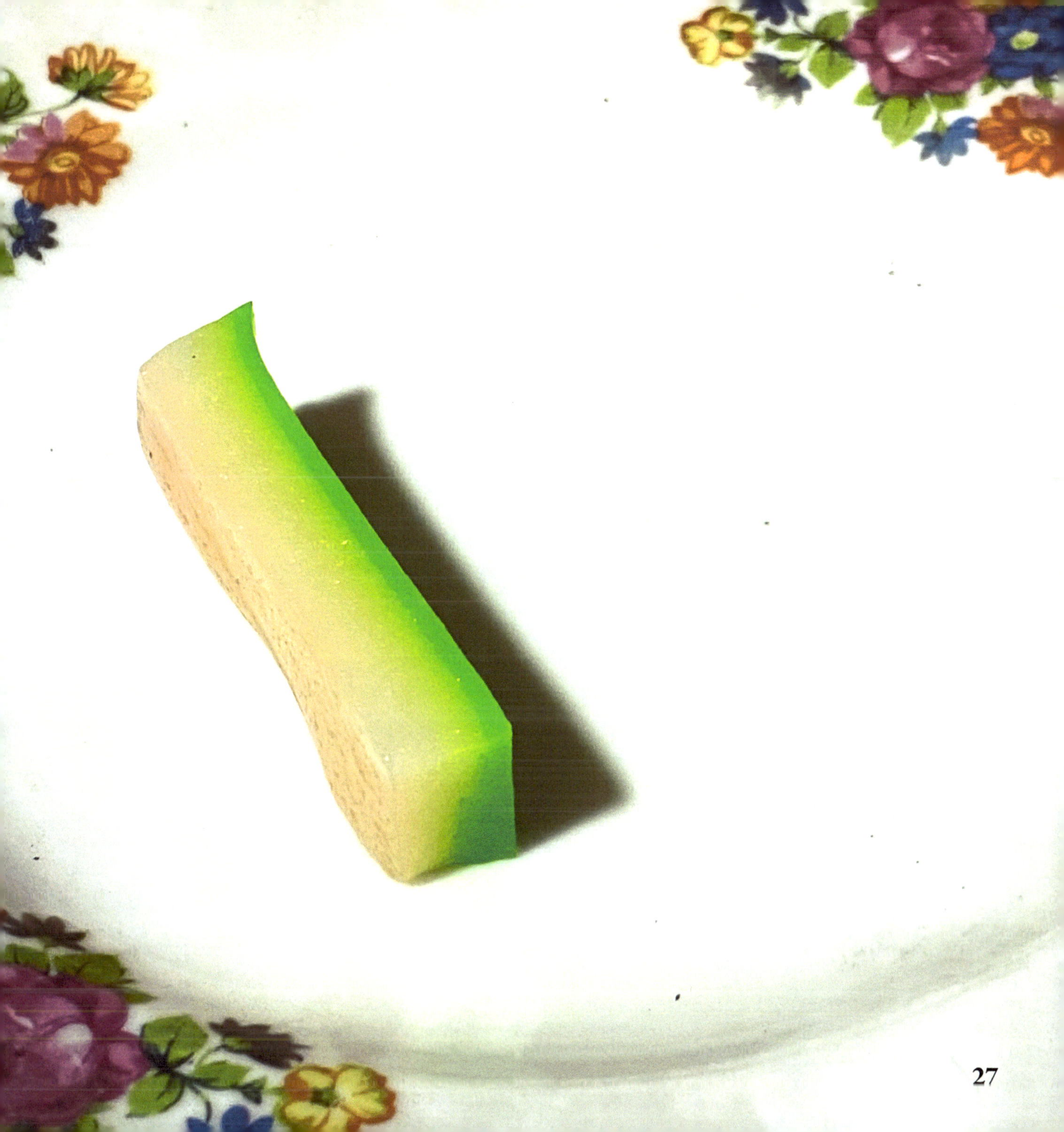

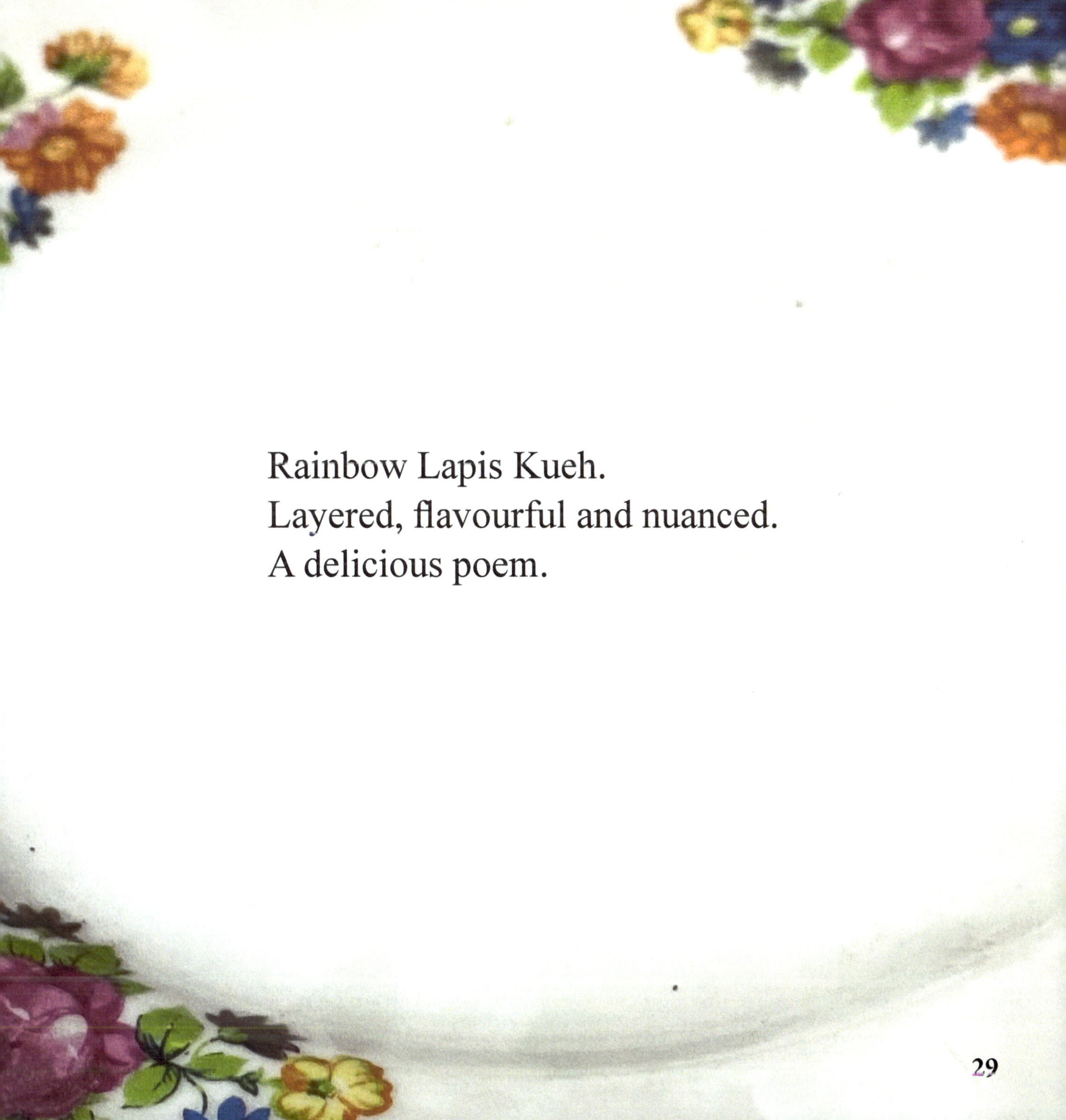

Rainbow Lapis Kueh.
Layered, flavourful and nuanced.
A delicious poem.

Sheng Mian / Crispy Noodles / A bed of crispy noodles topped with an assortment of meat and vegetables with a rich broth

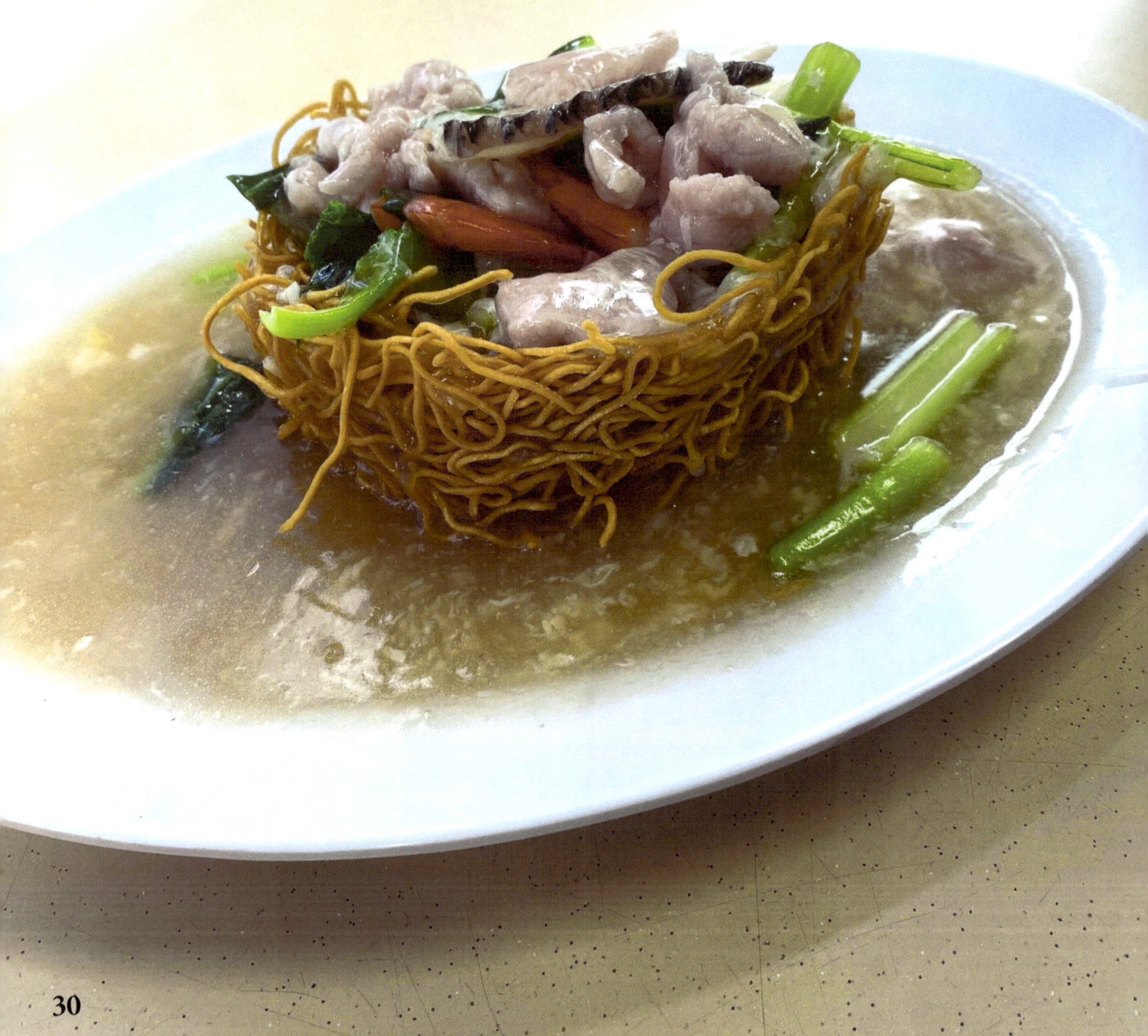

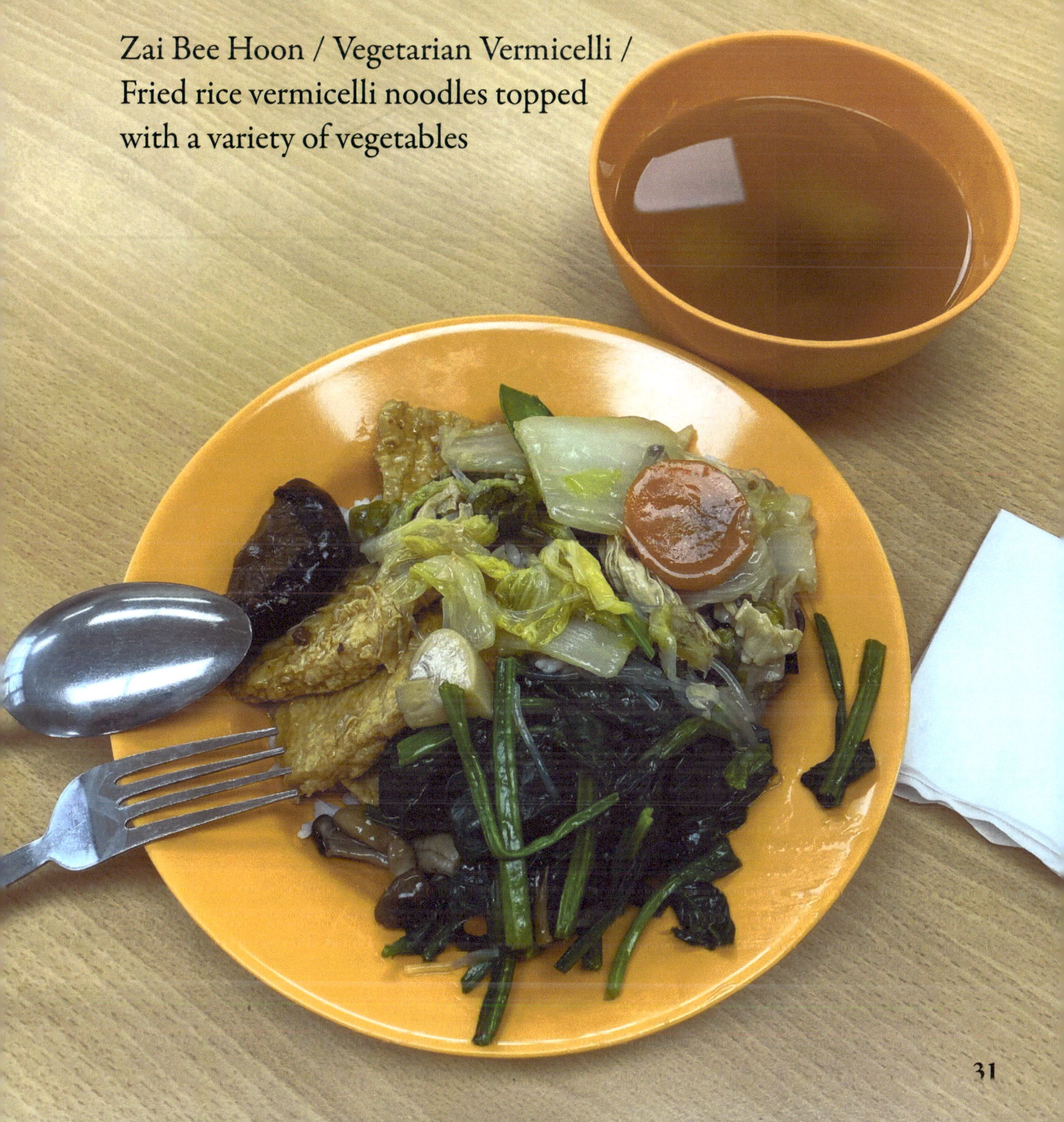
Zai Bee Hoon / Vegetarian Vermicelli /
Fried rice vermicelli noodles topped
with a variety of vegetables

31

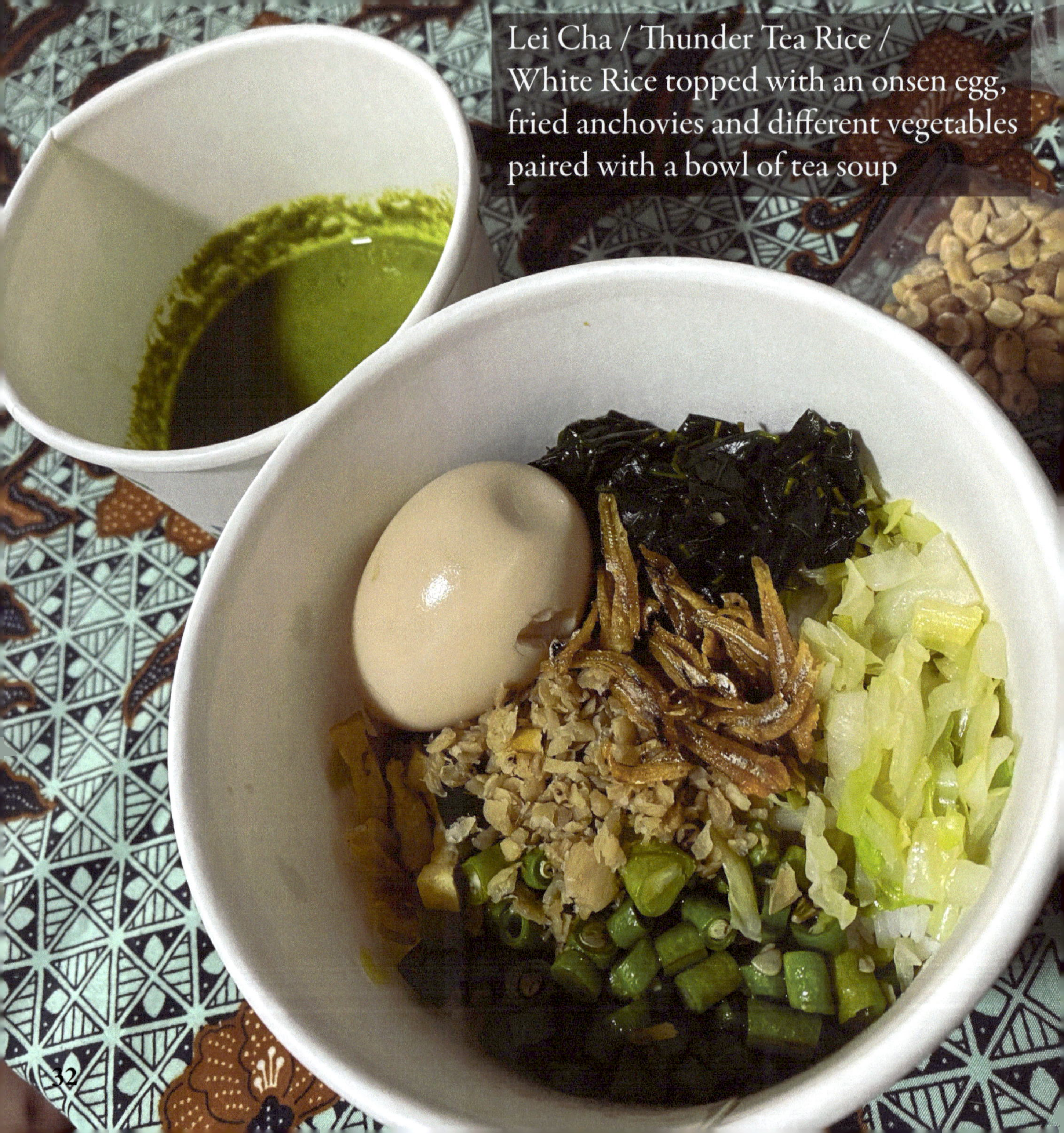

Lei Cha / Thunder Tea Rice /
White Rice topped with an onsen egg,
fried anchovies and different vegetables
paired with a bowl of tea soup

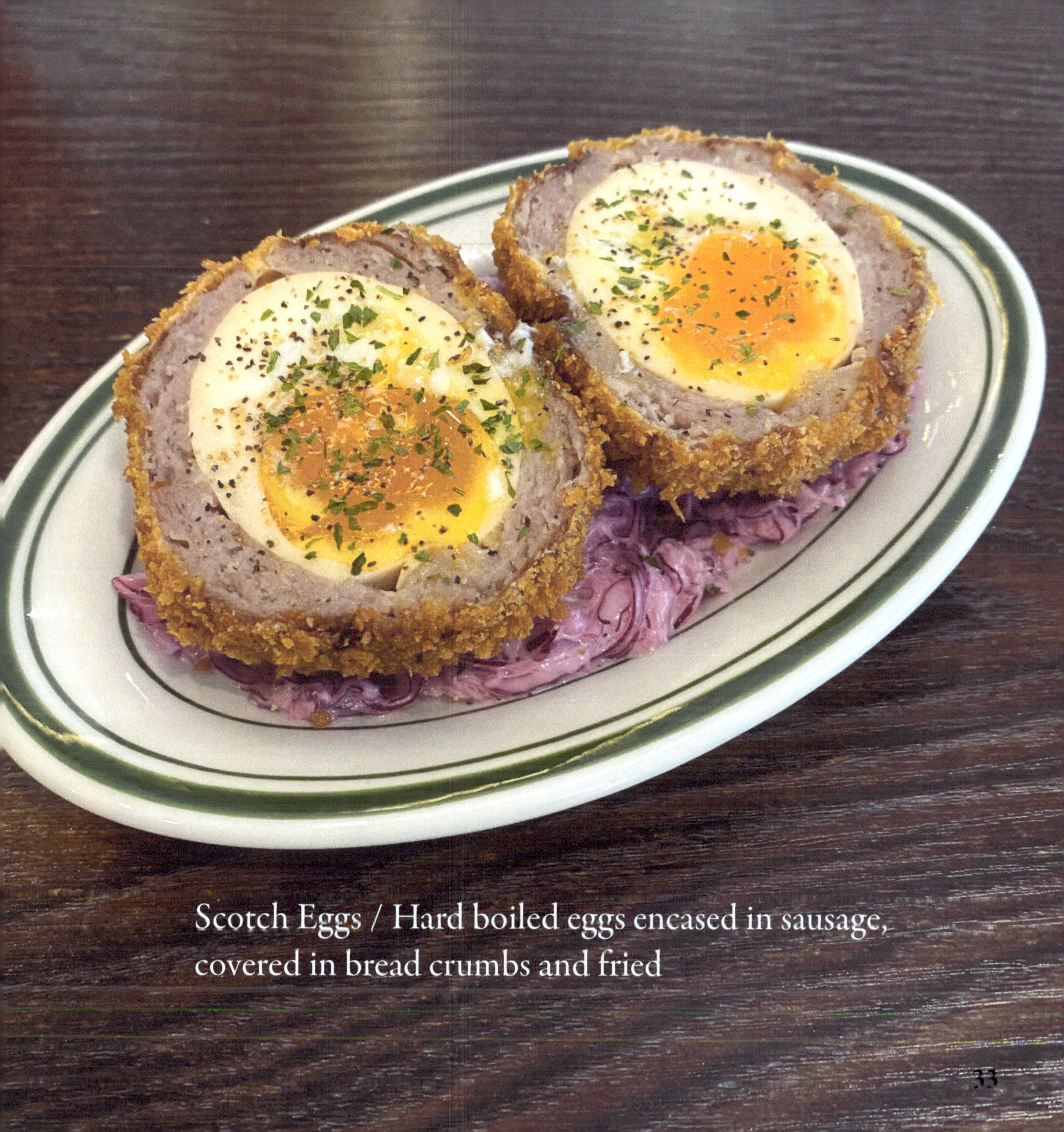

Scotch Eggs / Hard boiled eggs encased in sausage, covered in bread crumbs and fried

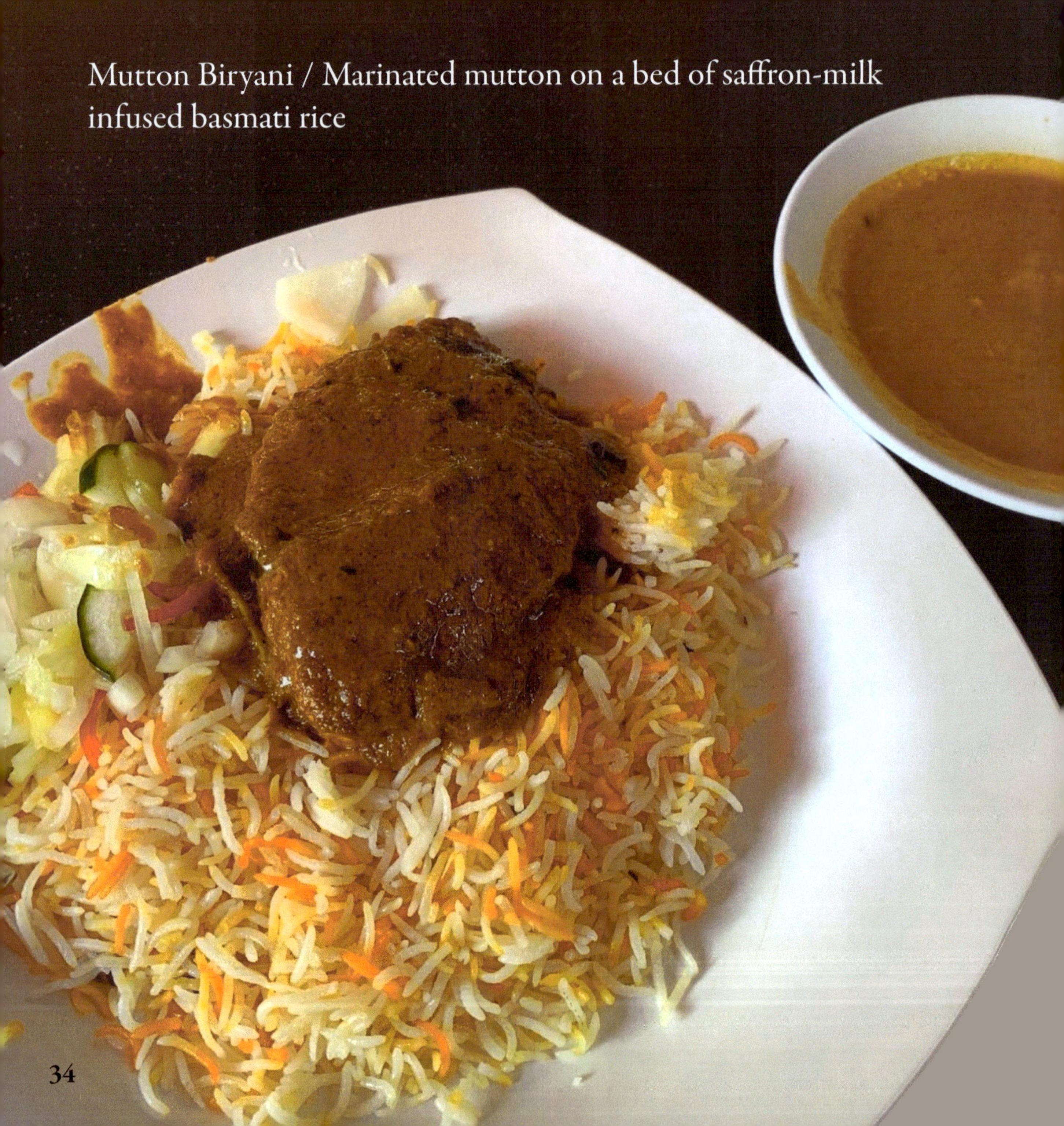

Mutton Biryani / Marinated mutton on a bed of saffron-milk infused basmati rice

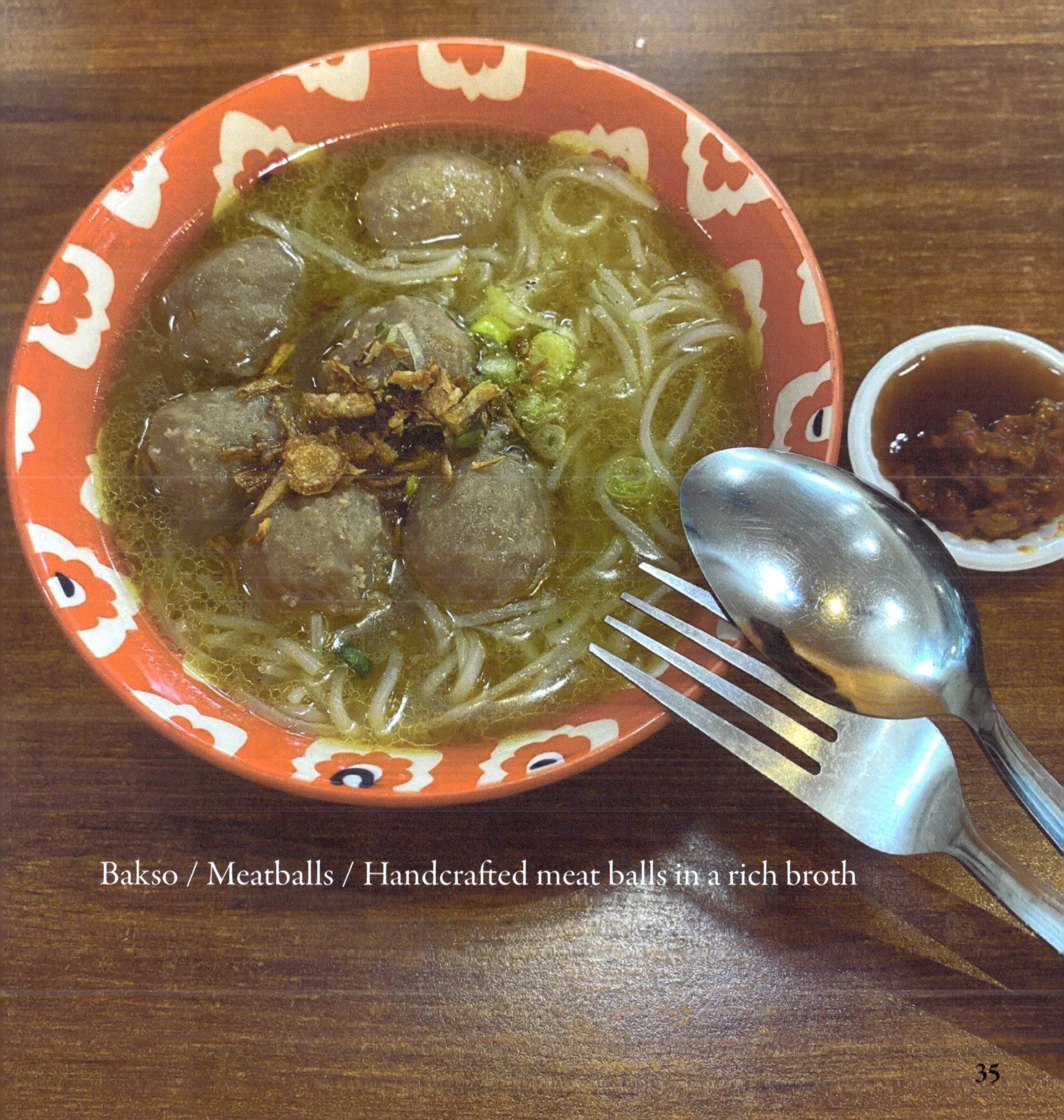

Bakso / Meatballs / Handcrafted meat balls in a rich broth

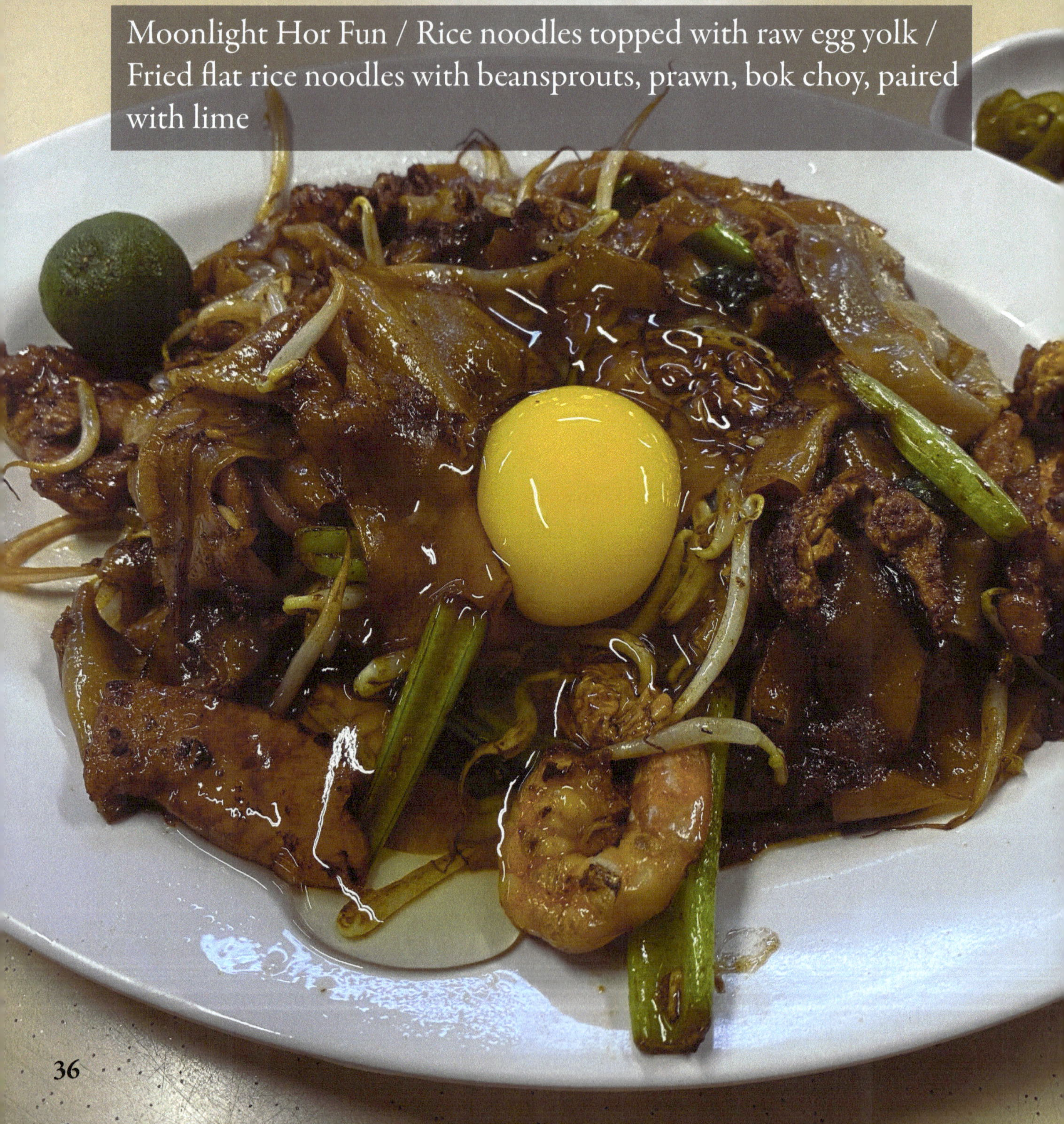
Moonlight Hor Fun / Rice noodles topped with raw egg yolk / Fried flat rice noodles with beansprouts, prawn, bok choy, paired with lime

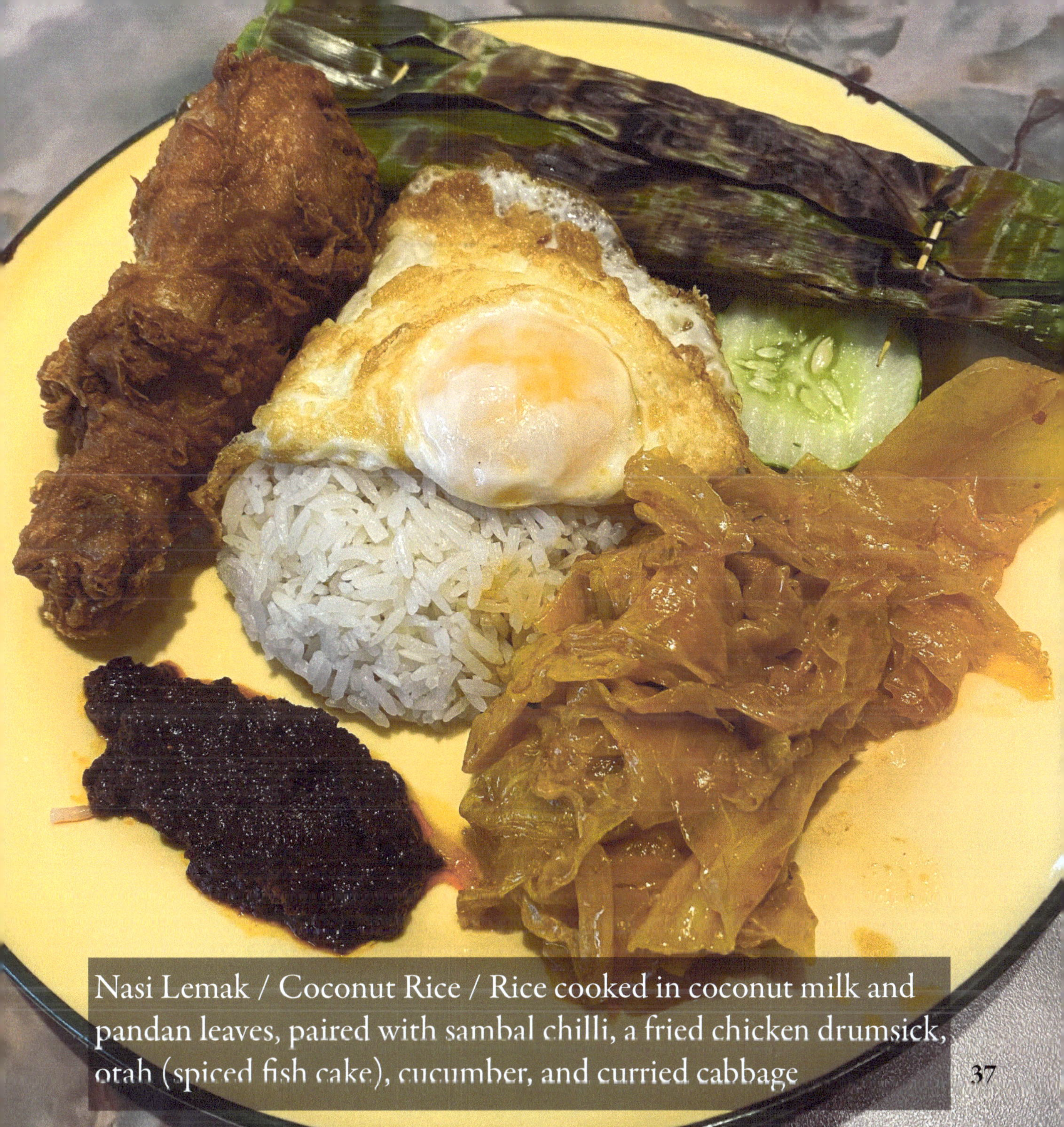

Nasi Lemak / Coconut Rice / Rice cooked in coconut milk and pandan leaves, paired with sambal chilli, a fried chicken drumsick, otah (spiced fish cake), cucumber, and curried cabbage

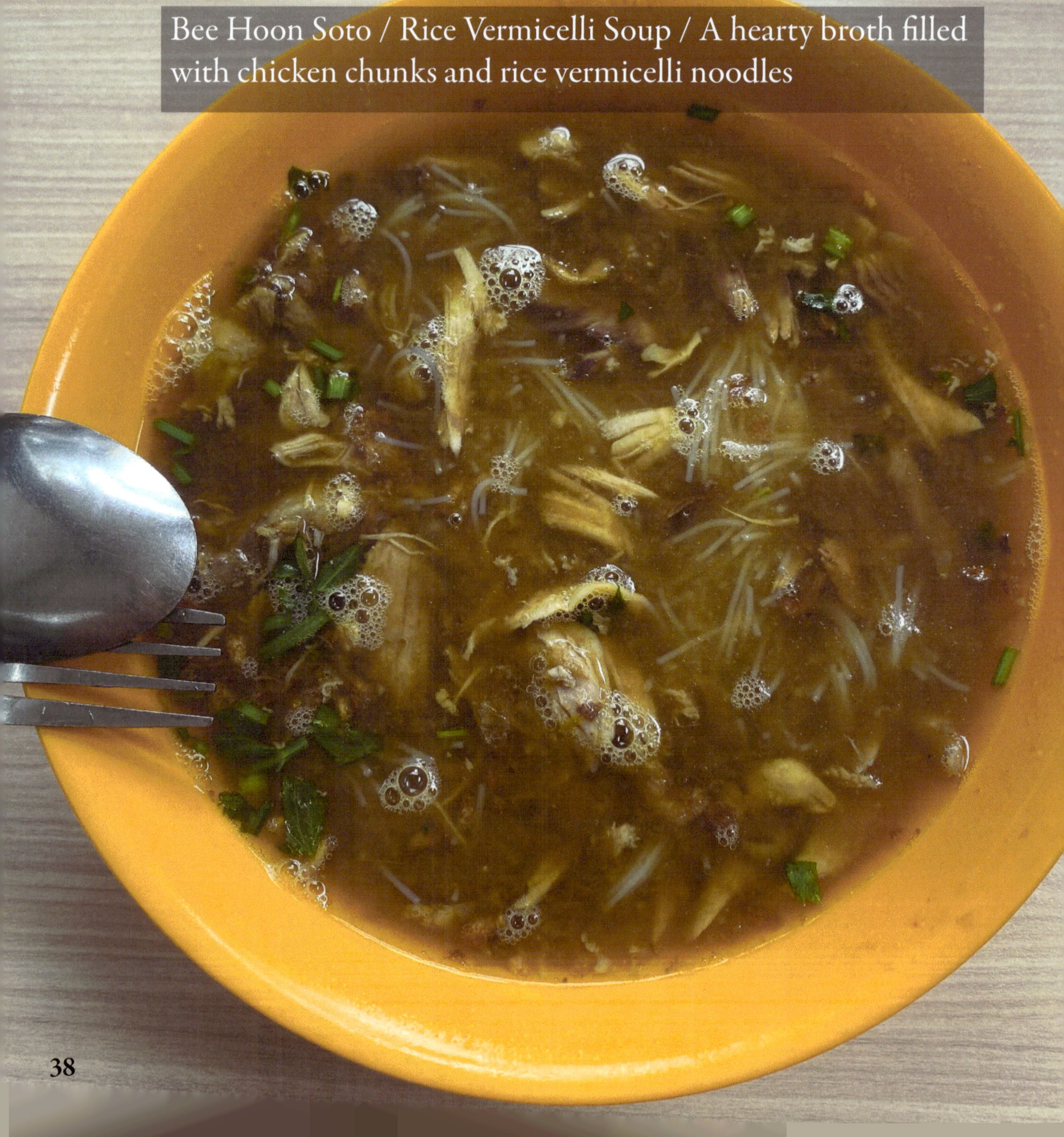
Bee Hoon Soto / Rice Vermicelli Soup / A hearty broth filled with chicken chunks and rice vermicelli noodles

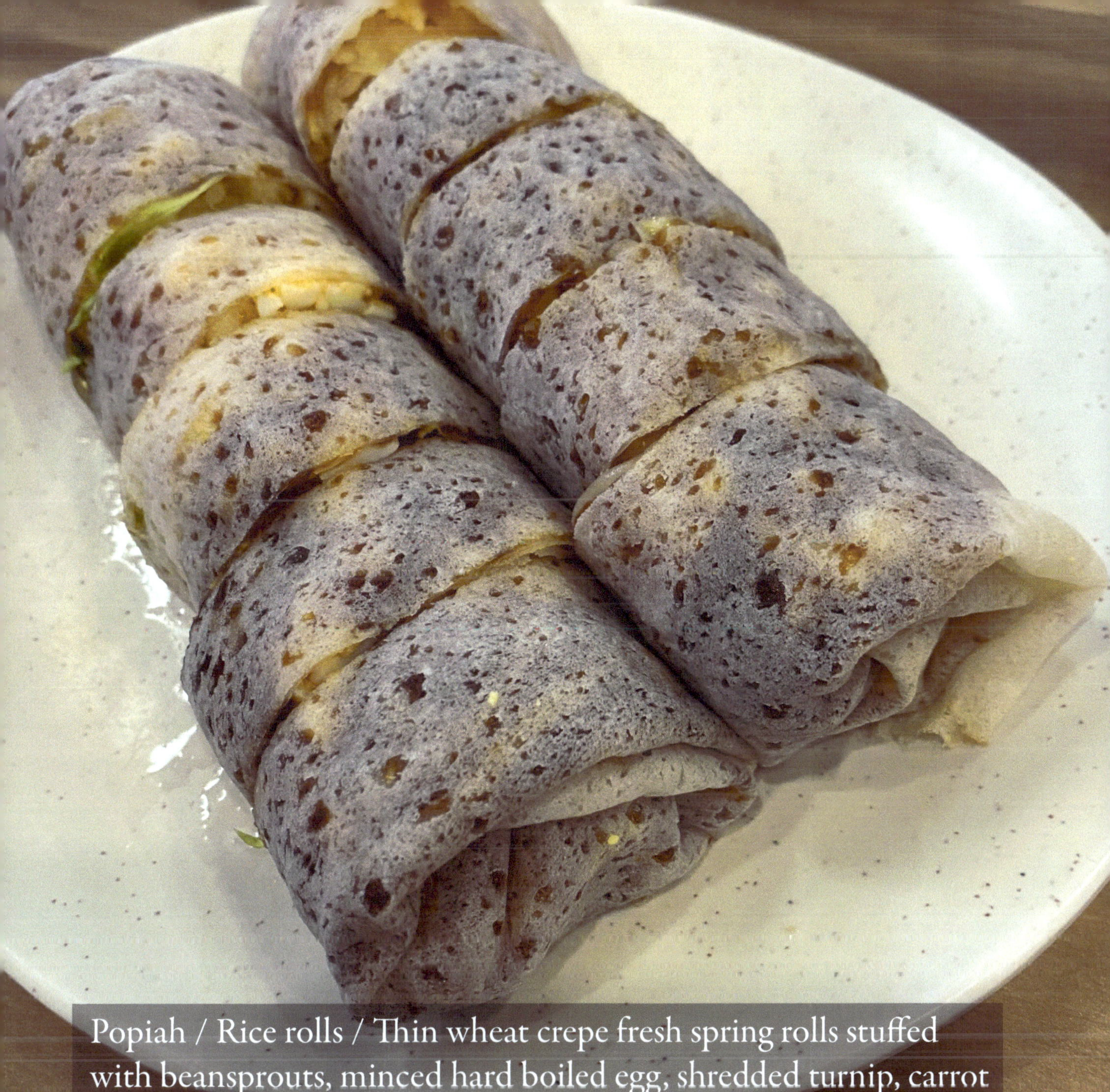

Popiah / Rice rolls / Thin wheat crepe fresh spring rolls stuffed
with beansprouts, minced hard boiled egg, shredded turnip, carrot
with sweet sauce and minced peanut

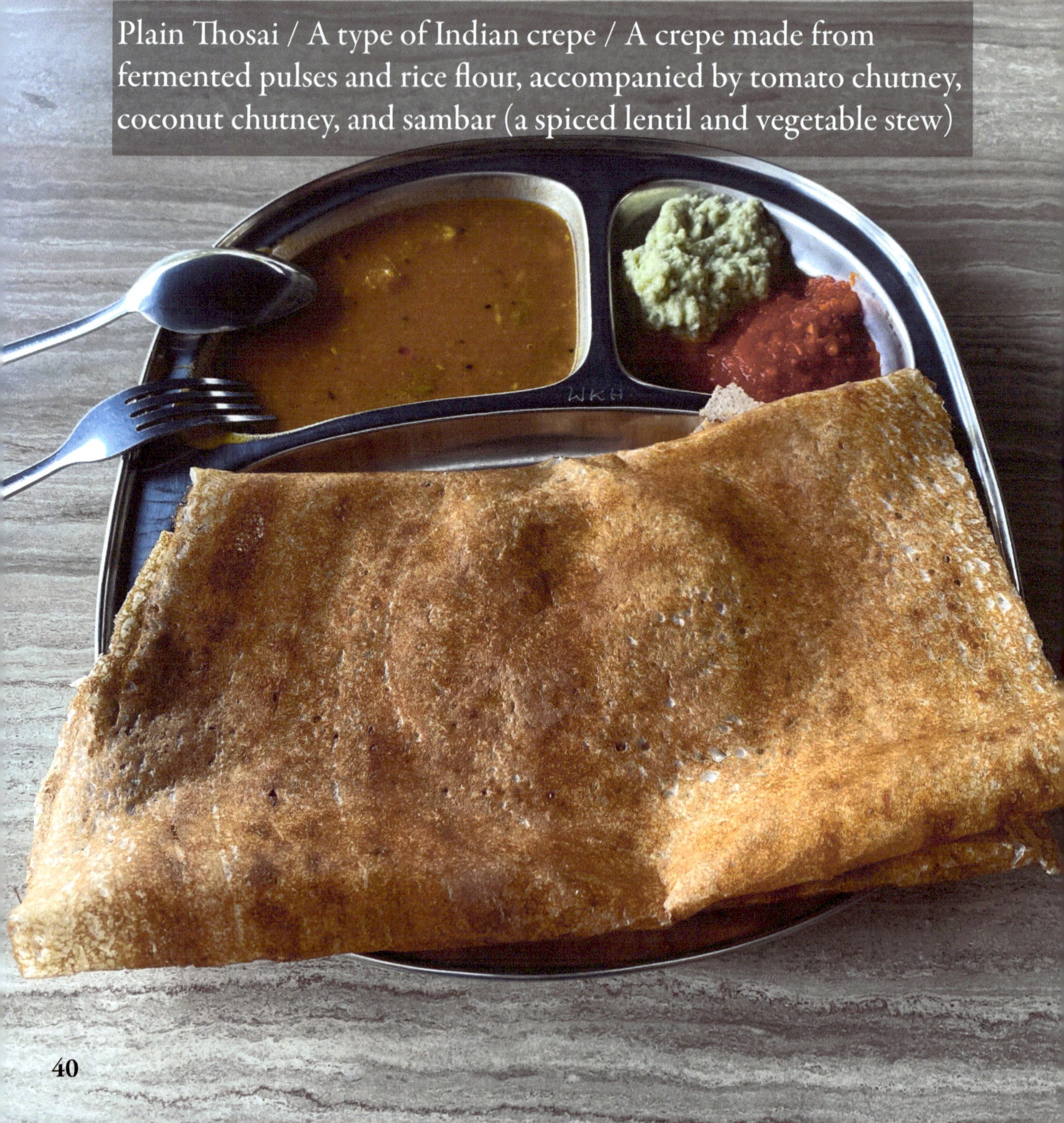

Plain Thosai / A type of Indian crepe / A crepe made from fermented pulses and rice flour, accompanied by tomato chutney, coconut chutney, and sambar (a spiced lentil and vegetable stew)

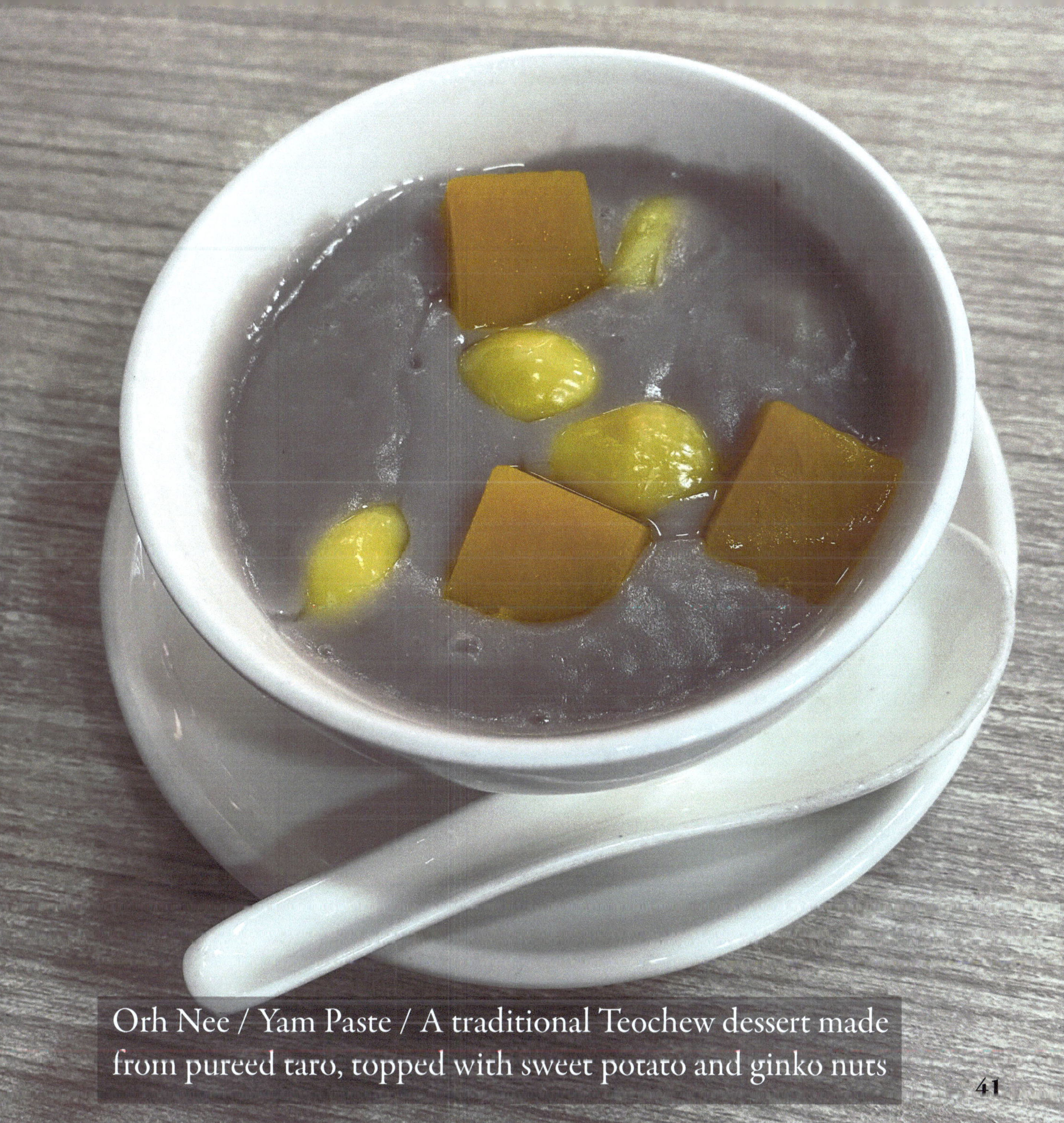

Orh Nee / Yam Paste / A traditional Teochew dessert made from pureed taro, topped with sweet potato and ginko nuts

41

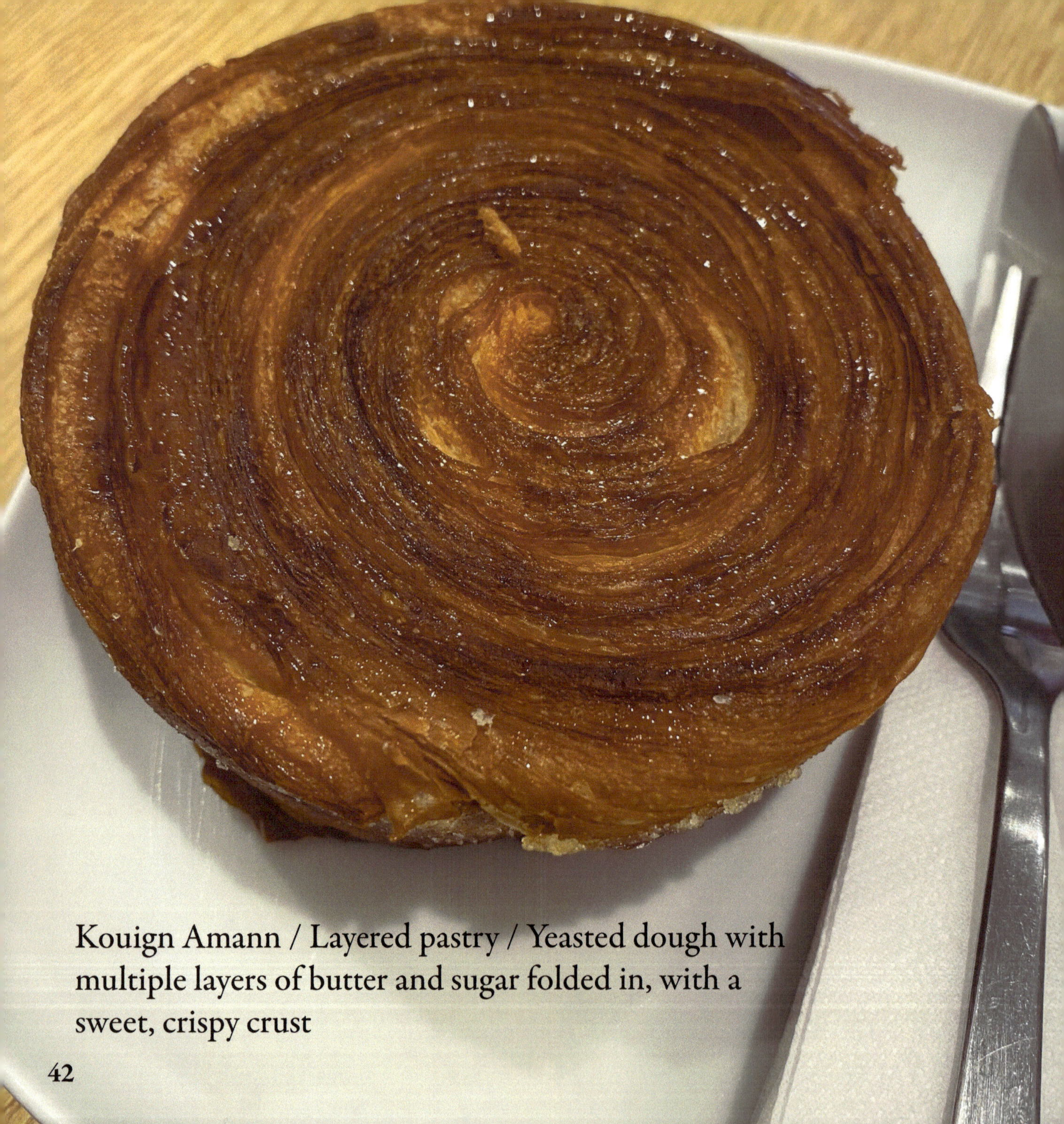

Kouign Amann / Layered pastry / Yeasted dough with multiple layers of butter and sugar folded in, with a sweet, crispy crust

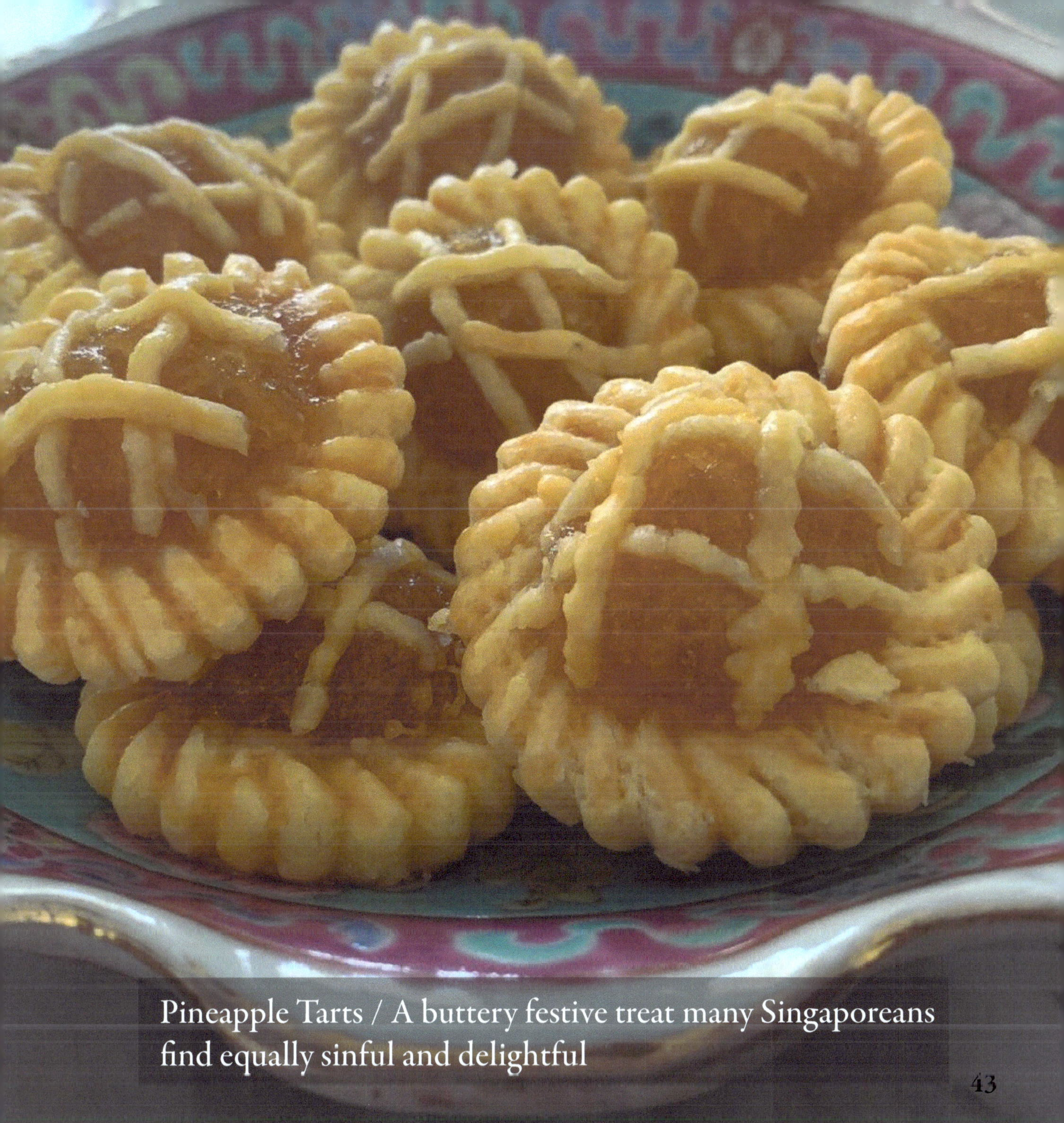

Pineapple Tarts / A buttery festive treat many Singaporeans find equally sinful and delightful

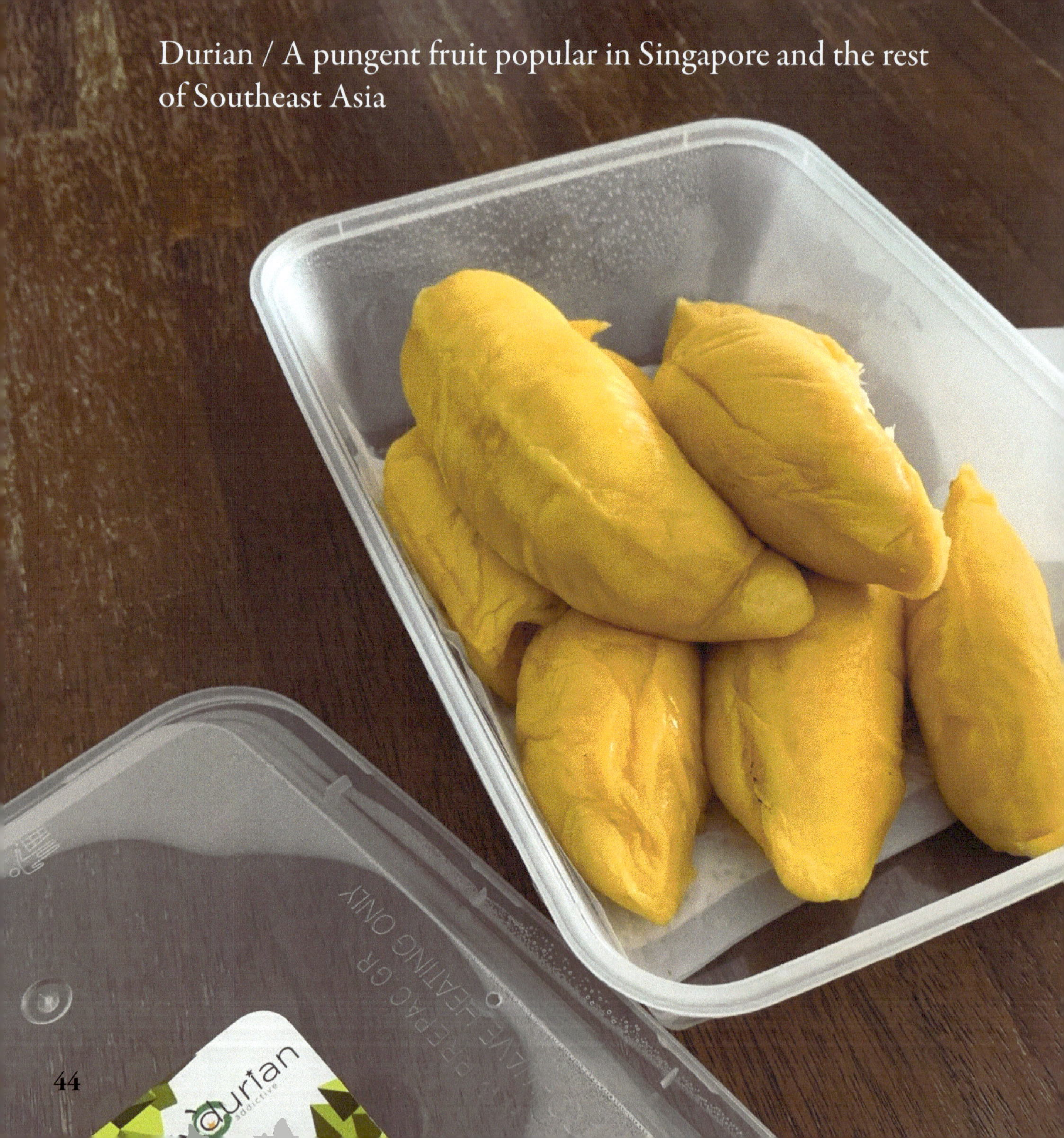

Durian / A pungent fruit popular in Singapore and the rest of Southeast Asia

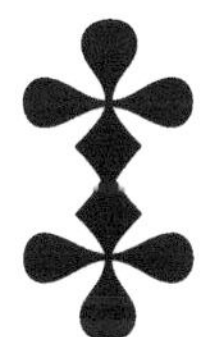

www.ingramcontent.com/pod-product-compliance
Lightning Source LLC
Chambersburg PA
CBHW041644110726

48005CB00003B/697